MW00332043

A ROYAL DUCHY

ABOVE *The arms of the Duchy of Cornwall. The supporters either side of the shield are Cornish choughs and the ostrich feathers of the Prince of Wales' feather badge. The shield is surmounted by the coronet of the Heir Apparent. The fifteen gold coins date back to the arms of the earls of Cornwall and represent the 'byzants' brought back by Crusaders from Byzantium. The motto 'Houmout' was used by the first Duke of Cornwall, the Black Prince, and translates as 'honour' or 'high-spirited'.*

FOLLOWING PAGE *Looking west across the valley of the River Fowey towards the ruins of Restormel Castle, Cornwall.*

Photographs by Peyto Slatter

THE DOVECOTE PRESS

A ROYAL DUCHY
A Portrait of the Duchy of Cornwall

DAVID BURNETT

First published in 1996 by The Dovecote Press Ltd
Stanbridge, Wimborne, Dorset BH21 4JD

1 3 5 7 9 10 8 6 4 2

ISBN 1 874336 39 3

Text © David Burnett 1996
Photographs © Peyto Slatter 1996
David Burnett has asserted his right under the Copyright, Designs and
Patents Act, 1988, to be identified as author of this work

Designed by Humphrey Stone

Typeset in Sabon by The Typesetting Bureau Ltd, Wimborne, Dorset
Origination and colour reproduction by Appletone Graphics, Bournemouth, Dorset
Printed by Broglia Press Ltd, Holton Heath, Poole, Dorset
Bound by Richard Harsher Ltd, Romsey, Hampshire

A CIP catalogue record for this book is available from the British Library

No part of this publication may be reproduced, stored in a retrieval system,
or transmitted, in any form or by any means without the prior permission
in writing of the publishers, nor be otherwise circulated in any form of
binding or cover other than that in which it is published and without
a similar condition including this condition being imposed
on the subsequent publisher.

All rights reserved

Contents

Maiden Castle, Dorset.

A Royal Duchy

As a boy, our family holidays were spent in Salcombe on a dismasted Brixham trawler that had been retired to calmer waters. On summer days, we slid head-first and screaming down the hole in the stern that had once held the rudder, scattering the mullet idling below. I did not know it then, but the handful of mud scooped from the sea-bed as proof we had reached it had a name, *fundus*, from the Latin for 'bottom', and legally it belonged to the Duchy of Cornwall.

That same ignorance about an institution apparently eager to claim ownership of river mud led another small boy to ask his mother how he was to earn a living when older. The boy was the young Edward VIII, who was told by Queen Mary that 'something' called the Duchy of Cornwall would look after him.

The Duchy of Cornwall has been taking care of princes since its foundation as a great landed estate in 1337 by Edward III to provide an income for the sovereign's eldest son, who becomes its duke on his birth or when a parent ascends the throne. It is the oldest dukedom in the country, but confusingly, and despite the title, only a small percentage of the Duchy is in Cornwall. Nearly seven centuries of history have played havoc with the lands first granted the Duchy. Much has been sold, some given away, new estates added. Today, the 129,000 acres that make up the Duchy of Cornwall are scattered over twenty-two counties, mostly in the West Country. Nearly half is farmed by more than 200 tenant farmers, the rest is woodland and unenclosed land on

LEFT *Salcombe and the Kingsbridge Estuary from the air, where the Duchy own both the foreshore and river bottom, or 'fundus'.*

Dartmoor. In addition, it owns nearly 1,100 houses, cottages, flats, offices, workshops, warehouses and small business units, virtually all of which are leased out or rented by others. Indeed the only businesses managed directly by the Duchy are the Duchy Nursery in Cornwall and the Home Farm at Highgrove, the Prince of Wales's Gloucestershire home. Finally there are its ancient rights to foreshore and river bottom, which bequeath it ownership of much of the Cornish and some of the South Devon foreshore between the high and low tide marks, and the navigable bed of eight of their rivers.

Such facts do it less than justice. There are castles, quarries and oyster beds; ancient woods and Iron Age hillforts. One farm might be a windswept few acres growing early daffodils on the Isles of Scilly, another a hop farm on the rim of the Malvern Hills. The commercial properties range from a Cornish fudge factory to jewellers' workshops in the heart of Birmingham, from Dartmoor Prison to the Oval cricket ground. The diversity owes much to the Duchy's medieval founder, who fashioned it around lands surplus to his needs and those he was willing to part with. This richness gives the Duchy its appeal. It also provides the present duke, the Prince of Wales, with a jigsaw of different landscapes, both rural and urban, to serve as a backdrop to his wishes that environmental and architectural concerns remain central to the way it is managed. The Duchy is England in miniature. It is also a kingdom in its own right, a dress rehearsal, which though governed by Parliament offers the Prince a stage on which to express his ideas and beliefs more effectively than likely when crowned king. Inner-city housing, an urban

The Duchy today. The photographs on this and the next three pages illustrate the diversity of its estates, and range from the Isles of Scilly to sheltered housing in Kennington.

LEFT *The Duchy on Dartmoor. The farm buildings looking out over the River Swincombe belong to Sherberton Farm, first mentioned in 1307, and a part of the Duchy since its foundation in 1337.*

OPPOSITE LEFT *The Isles of Scilly. A fishing boat passing Cromwell's Castle, Tresco, with Bryher in the background.*

OPPOSITE RIGHT *Stowcastle Street, Poundbury, where the Duchy is involved in building an extension to the Dorset town of Dorchester.*

OPPOSITE LOWER RIGHT *Tresco Court, Sancroft Street, Kennington.*

OPPOSITE *The map shows the West Country, where most – though not all – of the Duchy's land holdings are centred. Today, the Duchy owns approximately 129,000 acres in twenty-two counties. The main holdings are:*

Cambridgeshire	*1,186*
Cornwall	*20,578*
Devon	*72,358*
Dorset	*3,370*
Gloucestershire	*2,196*
Greater London	*35*
Herefordshire	*1,885*
Isles of Silly	*3,975*
Lincolnshire	*1,935*
Nottinghamshire	*714*
Somerset	*16,385*
South Glamorgan	*711*
Wiltshire	*3,746*

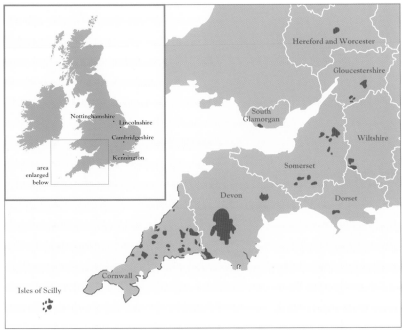

ABOVE *Autumn colours on Duchy farmland at Cradley in Herefordshire.*

RIGHT *Duchy foreshore in North Cornwall: Trebarwith Strand, just south of Tintagel Castle.*

extension to a Dorset town, moorland farms, a cluster of islands on the rim of the Atlantic, all bear the same landlord as the rolling lowland landscapes that typify so much of the Duchy.

Nor can the Prince stand accused of squandering his opportunities. When in his twenties he first became involved in the Duchy's affairs it was well-intentioned but old-fashioned. Royal patronage invested an air of privilege. The great weight of its history made it cumbersome and slow to change. The cobwebs have long since been blown away. Again and again the Prince has chivvied and cajoled it into going in directions that once would have been unthinkable. Of all the great landowning estates, it is by far the most dynamic, even the most radical. Conservation, architecture, organic farming, the conversion of redundant buildings into workshops, landscape surveys – each of these is central to its management and policies.

The Duchy's London headquarters are in Buckingham Gate. Prints of the now ruined castles that once welded the estates together line the mustard yellow walls of the octagonal hall. During the winter, the narcissi sent weekly from Scilly bring a splash of spring to the half-landing on the stairs. If Prince Charles is the Duchy's 'chairman', then its 'managing director' is its Secretary and Keeper of the Records, Jimmy James, whose first-floor room looks out towards Buckingham Palace. There are bookcases, portraits, rolled-up plans, a desk strewn with papers – an air of comfortable elegance. The Prince is advised by a Prince's Council that meets four times a year, either at Highgrove, or in its Chamber adjoining the Secretary's room. Invitations to join the Council remain the prerogative of the Prince, each member bringing skills that reflect the Duchy's diversity. Three are earls, a fourth a Cornish landowner. One is the Prince's Private Secretary, another is Second Commissioner of the Crown Estate and on the Council of the Duchy of Lancaster. The odd man out is a non-Duchy tenant farmer from Exmoor, whose broad Devonian vowels bring a welcome touch of less favoured worlds.

Altogether the Duchy employs fewer than a hundred people. Jimmy James's Deputy, Kevin Knott, is responsible for its financial management. Tim Gray, the Estate Surveyor, looks after the commercial portfolio and what remains of the Kennington

10 Buckingham Gate, designed by Sir James Pennethorne, and the headquarters of the Duchy of Cornwall since 1857.

estate. Kiloran McGrigor has risen through the ranks of the secretarial staff in Buckingham Palace to be its Press Officer, a role grown ever more daunting as the Duchy's activities have broadened. There is an accounts department and professional secretariat. There is also an archivist, for the Duchy's library and archives are amongst its greatest treasures, and their contents range from a fourteenth century legal text-book to medieval court rolls, as well as the correspondence and accounts stored in successive muniment rooms.

But the bulk of those on the payroll are not based in London at all, but in the offices of its three Land Stewards – in Somerset, Cornwall, and the Isles of Scilly. As well as its Land Steward, the Scillonian staff includes a Harbour Master. The Cornish office in Liskeard covers the Western District of Cornwall, Dartmoor, and south Devon. All the land east of Exeter is contained within the Eastern District. The Land Stewards running the mainland estates are assisted by a pair of deputies, who help deal with tenants on a day-to-day basis; whilst Dartmoor's peculiar status has rewarded it with a separate office in Princetown, again headed by a Deputy Land Steward.

Together with the farmers and other tenants, these are the people whose hard work last year rewarded the Prince of Wales with an income from the Duchy before tax of about £5 million. They are also the people whose willingness to talk about their work and the land in their care helped make this book possible. Of course the Duchy has faults. Few encounters with farmers failed to begin without a suspicious silence, lest I be either a tax collector or tabloid journalist, turning into a complaint about the rent, a characteristic bred into tenant farmers as surely as the mud in their yards. Grievances once aired, no community could have been more welcoming. Rams were paraded, corn sampled, fields walked. Gradually it transpired that neighbouring tenants of other institutional landowners regarded the Duchy as less impersonal and much fairer in its dealings. More than one made it clear he would rather be bossed around by England's future king than a bank or pension fund.

Despite their concern that the turbulence surrounding Prince Charles's private life might in some way affect them, most tenant farmers are genuinely fond of their landlord, patting the sofa where he had sat on a visit, fetching the framed photograph taken before his departure. Many felt themselves part of an extended family whose triumphs and tragedies touch their lives more directly than the rest of us. One farmer's wife came close to tears when mentioning the break-up of the Prince's marriage. Others spoke of hand-written letters he had sent them on the death of a father, of Christmas cards, presents, invitations to garden parties at Buckingham Palace or Highgrove.

But if the Prince is not immune to the occasional grumble, usually about the viability of organic farming, nor is the Duchy itself. Its hierarchical structure and inbuilt cautiousness can make decision-making slow. Most criticism comes from Dartmoor and the Isles of Scilly, areas overlooked by the Duchy in the past and whose wider economic futures remain less assured. The Poundbury development at Dorchester, where the Duchy is involved in the most ambitious building project in its history, is not without controversy.

Yet such complaints acquire perspective when measured against the range of the Duchy's achievements. Except for a few years following the Civil War, it has picked its way through seven centuries of change, staying true to its purpose and traditions, adapting when necessary, steering a course through shifting political tides.

Princes may rule it, but its bedrock are the ordinary men and women who work the land. Many Duchy farms have been tenanted by successive generations of the same family, adding to its sense of continuity. To me, this kinship with the land in their care reflected a set of values and traditions that form one of the Duchy's greatest strengths, and which we cast aside at our peril. One such farm is Wardbrook, a 960 acre holding on the flank of Bodmin Moor. The farm has been part of the Duchy since its foundation, and is now tenanted by Michael and Margaret Hooper. A rough track winds uphill past the standing stones raised by earlier settlers. The farm straddles the 1,000 feet contour, and its buildings look out over rough grazing, bog, and a ring of granite-topped tors. Snow can lie until May, mist roll in without warning. The sleepers of a long abandoned railway that once carried stone from a nearby quarry still run through the farmyard. Michael and Margaret were twenty-two and nineteen

Michael Hooper and his daughter, Elaine, rounding-up cattle at Wardbrook Farm on the edge of Bodmin Moor.

Ian Piper at Bearah Tor Quarry.

when they took on the tenancy in 1975. Wardbrook is their lives, the Duchy a distant landlord that only rarely ventures onto the Moor. Both husband and wife shepherd their flock of Scottish Blackface sheep and home-bred Galloway cattle. In the early days, Margaret wrapped her three children, then all under five, in hot-water bottles and took them out onto the Moor in an old Landrover, retreating to its warmth to feed the youngest. So steep are the slopes and many the boulders that even today Michael does much of the farm work on horseback.

Not far from Wardbrook is Bearah Tor Quarry, a Duchy quarry that after closing at the end of the nineteenth century reopened in the 1930s when Clifford Piper took the tenancy. Today Bearah Tor is let to his son Ian. The sixteen masons employed by his father have dwindled to two. An ancient cast-iron hand crane built within twenty years of the Crimean War towers over piles of rubble stone. Little has changed since its

arrival. The three ton granite blocks are split using tools a medieval mason would have carried. Water plays on a diamond-tipped fifty-year-old saw slowly cutting stone into slabs. A line of chisels sit beside the forge awaiting tempering and resharpening. Much of the work is restoration: church towers, carving, patching up country houses.

In June 1995, in driving rain, a convoy of Range Rovers carrying Prince Charles in its midst bumped its way up the two mile track leading to the quarry, a destination described by one Duchy official as the 'back-of-beyond'. The weather was appalling, shortening the visit. Yet to me, as when watching Michael Hooper check his flock from the saddle, Bearah Tor's remoteness gave the Duchy a focus no explanation could hope to compete with. Suddenly it had a purpose not measured in money, but became a symbol of something older, more enduring – a world and way of life worth preserving.

From Black Prince to Prince of Wales

On a February morning in 1337 Edward III, 'a wreath on his head, a ring on his finger', lowered a silver wand onto the shoulder of his eldest son, Prince Edward of Woodstock. It was a ceremony shot through with medieval splendour. Ranged round him in Westminster's great hall were forty knights, their ladies beside them, who promised to remove the silk covering one eye only after performing some knightly deed. When the ceremony ended, the six-year-old prince had an income, estates, and a new title – Duke of Cornwall. Although history remembers him as the Black Prince, the adjective was not used during his lifetime, and probably refers to his complexion or the colour of the armour he wore at Crécy and Poitiers.

Edward III's motives for granting England's first dukedom to his heir mixed political expediency with practical commonsense. Still only twenty-four, the hazards of kingship had long since taught him realism. His father had been murdered. His mother and her lover had led England into civil war. The Scots under Robert the Bruce had laid waste much of the north. The vast French landholdings built-up by successive English kings had gradually been dissipated.

Edward III's greatest strengths were an instinctive shrewdness and sure political touch. The death in the previous year of his younger brother, the Earl of Cornwall, had returned to the crown an immense West Country estate first formed following the Saxon conquest of Cornwall in the tenth century. The Cornish hankering for independence had never died. By retaining the earldom for himself he risked alienating its people still further. The elevation from earldom to dukedom, and the gift of

The Black Prince (1330-1376), the first Duke of Cornwall, paying homage to his father, Edward III.

it to his son, might appeal to Cornish pride and give the illusion that they were being granted some semblance of autonomy from direct English rule. Most importantly, its revenues would provide the heir to a cash-starved throne with a substantial additional income.

Edward III also knew that the monarchy was at its weakest when the succession was uncertain, a question the charter founding the new duchy sought to resolve by stating that only the monarch's first-born son could become Duke of Cornwall. If no duke existed, the title reverted to the crown. Thus only he who held the Duchy could succeed to the throne. This belt and braces approach to the dynastic struggles that tore apart the medieval monarchy was further tightened by one other statute. The entire Duchy was to be handed over intact by one duke to the next. Each could spend its income, but not the capital. Not all Edward III's successors have honoured this condition.

Launceston Castle, Cornwall.

Extravagance, debt, gifts to favourites, the filling of coffers to wage war, indifference, incompetence – all have played their part in reducing the modern Duchy to much less than its original size.

The core of the estate granted to the young prince had been pieced together following the Norman conquest, when William I made his half-brother Earl of Cornwall. The first earl built castles at Trematon and Launceston, strategically sited to control the main routes into the county. A later earl, Richard, King of the Romans, added to his coat-of-arms fifteen gold coins, the 'byzants' brought back by Crusaders from Byzantium, that still adorn those of the Duchy today. Near the River Fowey in Lostwithiel, his son built a range of buildings to meet the administrative needs of the earldom: its court, exchequer, shire hall and prison.

All of these, together with seventeen Cornish manors, were granted to the new Duchy. Edward III was determined to create an estate to match his son's status, and over the next few years enlarged it still further with land in fifteen other counties, ranging from the 60,000 acre Forest of Dartmoor in the west to a group of manors round Knaresborough in the north. The 18,000 acre Soke of Kirton-in-Lindsey on the Lincolnshire fens, with its two towns and thirty-nine villages, became part of the Duchy, as did the tiny Sussex manor of Old Shoreham. The castles of Rougemont in Exeter, Rysing in Norfolk, Rockingham in Northamptonshire, as well as Wallingford and Berkhamsted, provided the new duke with fortresses loyal to the crown. There were lands in Somerset and Dorset, the city of Coventry, the Honour of Mere in Wiltshire, and south of the Thames in then rural Surrey, the manor of Kennington, where in due course the Black Prince made his home.

From each corner of this scattered dukedom came the revenues required by the prince. A seventeenth-century Cornishman grown weary of the ways by which the Duchy extracted money, wrote, ' . . . tribute was imposed upon everything of profit . . . for corporations, fairs, market, taking or freeing from tolls, mines, fishing, fowling, hawking, hunting and what not . . .'. The last phrase is the most telling, for the list could have lengthened indefinitely. Harbour dues were levied on all ships in need of an anchorage in ports controlled by the Duchy. Every ship of under

Kingsand, on the west bank of Plymouth Sound. The fish cellars on the foreshore beyond the houses were built in the sixteenth century by the merchants of Plymouth to evade tax on pilchards landed in Plymouth.

greyhound a year: by 1590 the tenancy was fifty greyhounds in arrears. A cottager near Constantine annually baked a lamprey and raisin pie in lieu of rent, a Somerset tenant armed with a bow and a dozen arrows had to accompany the duke whenever he entered the county.

The Duchy was administered and its income collected by an elaborate hierarchy of paid officials, some of whose titles are still preserved in the modern Duchy. There were bailiffs, reeves, stewards, auditors, receivers, even a Havener, or 'keeper of the waters of the King's ports in Cornwall'. Some of these posts were given by the Black Prince to those who had fought at his side in France; men such as William Lenche, his porter, who after losing an eye at Poitiers was rewarded with the income from a ferry over the Tamar. At the apex of this pyramid was another of the Black Prince's creations to survive, a group of advisers called the Prince's Council. Of these, the most important member was the Lord Warden of the Stannaries, a title derived from the tin-mining districts in Devon and Cornwall. The Stannaries (from *stannum*, the Latin for 'tin') were a special jurisdiction with their own courts, and pre-date the Duchy. Edward III assigned the Duchy their profits, and for the next 500 years it was they that provided the Duchy with the lion's share of its income.

The tin trade dominated the medieval south-west. One in ten Cornishmen was involved in the industry. Nearly a thousand tinworks and processing mills have been identified on Dartmoor alone. Prospectors, miners and smelters all gathered wherever the tin-rich surface ore in a river valley or stream bed could easily be worked. The tin was smelted into ingots and taken to one of the eight Stannary towns; Launceston, Lostwithiel, Truro and Helston in Cornwall, and Tavistock, Chagford, Ash-burton and Plympton in Devon. These were the only towns where it could legally be sold, and on Coinage Days they filled with tin-laden pack-horses, officials, tin dealers, pewter factors, Flemish and Italian merchants. Each block of tin was formally weighed, sampled – or 'coigned', from the French for 'corner' – by the assay master clipping off a corner, then stamped with the owner's name, and the coinage dues paid on it.

To protect its profits, the crown had established a system of rights and privileges to govern the industry. The tinners were

20 tons landing wine in those ports was obliged to hand over a cask, or two if its tonnage was greater. The goods of those who died without heirs automatically became Duchy property: this right, known as *bona vacantia*, still survives, though at the present Prince of Wales's request any receipts are now handed over to the Duke of Cornwall's Benevolent Fund. The Right of Wreck allowed it to claim shipwrecks and whales washed ashore. Even the smallest harbour was liable to customs dues, with one, Portwrinkle, continuing to be charged for all pilchards landed on its quay as late as the 1780s. Anyone wishing to fish the Duchy-owned Cornish and Devon rivers, or their estuaries, had first to pay. Nor was it only money that changed hands. The holder of one Cornish manor was obliged to part with one

The ruined twelfth century keep of Lydford Castle, once the site of a Stannary prison.

The ruins of Berkhamsted Castle. When in England, the Duchy of Cornwall's first duke, the Black Prince, divided his time between either the castle or his palace in Kennington.

fiercely independent, and allowed freedoms unthinkable elsewhere. They were spared military service, free to dig peat and divert rivers. As well as holding their own parliaments, they were tried in their own courts. Those found guilty were imprisoned in the Stannary gaols at Lostwithiel and Lydford, where, so ran the rhyme, 'in the morn they hang and draw, and sit in judgement after'.

The threat of such a fate helped the Black Prince retain a grip on what was undoubtedly the unruliest part of the Duchy. One Bishop of Exeter, enthroned ten years before the Duchy's creation, described the south-western peninsula as, 'not only the ends of the earth, but the very ends of the ends thereof'. Dartmoor was wilderness, Cornwall poor in everything but tin and fish. Most of the Duchy's Cornish holdings were of less than 30 acres, with the small granite-edged fields that are still a feature of the landscape. The constant draining of wealth by innumerable dues fuelled resentment. The miners grew adept at avoiding payment, smuggling tin down-river hidden under barrels of fish.

The character of the Black Prince is so obscured by 'the fair and noble prince' of the battlefield he remains difficult to pin down. War was his world, and it was war that increasingly preoccupied him, first in France, where he ruled a second principality, Aquitaine, then Spain. He married late, aged thirty-one, choosing as his bride the twice-married Joan of Kent, the 'fair maid of Kent', after whose blue riband, dropped at a ball, the Order of the Garter had been named. Whilst in England he divided his time between Kennington Palace and the now ruined castle of Berkhamsted on the slopes of the Chilterns. From the great palace he had built at Kennington, with its vineyard, chapel, and long hall lined with black Purbeck marble columns, he looked out over farmland and meadows. Nothing survives. Henry VIII demolished the palace to provide materials for his own palace in Whitehall. London's southward march during the nineteenth century swept away the nurseries and market gardens then occupying the meadows. The Black Prince's financial base and exchequer were north of the Thames in Fish Mill Street, closer to Westminster. Within two hundred years of his death it was a cheap tavern called the Black Belle, and was finally engulfed by the Fire of London.

In 1349 the Black Death reached Devon and Cornwall, bringing tin production to a standstill. The impact of the plague caused bewilderment and hardship. Villages lacking churchyards carried their dead away at night by the cart-load. Of the 74 tenants at Stoke Climsland, close to the Tamar, only six survived. The poverty the disease left behind reinforce contemporary descriptions of the Black Prince as a landlord who 'cared for his tenants, comforting them in many ways.' Rather than leave land abandoned, rents stayed uncollected. Tinners unable to pay coinage dues were allowed to pay smaller fines rather than forfeit their tin. One year his steward was ordered to round-up the deer grazing Dartmoor, 'both harts and hindes', and divide them amongst those whose crops they had most damaged. Nor can his devotion be questioned. Timber was given for repairs to Stoke Climsland church, to the friars in Truro, to the Prior of Tywardreath. If his wish to found a chantry at Tintagel Castle, where a chaplain would pray for the souls of his ancestors, was thwarted by the site's bleakness and the size of the salary offered, he was more successful elsewhere. The offer of an increase to his fifty shilling salary persuaded Sir William Pruett to promise to spend the rest of his life singing daily masses in a hermitage in Restormel Park.

Yet there are contradictions. The enigmatic request to his Cornish steward that 'he do right' in harvesting the revenues from tin are a reminder of the costs of waging war, costs the Cornish all too often had to meet. From Plymouth went ships laden with men, horses, salt fish and bundles of arrows. In the summer of 1354, when on his first visit to Cornwall to board a ship for France, lack of wind becalmed his fleet for six weeks, during which period the Duchy's Cornish tenants kept his household in wine and wheat.

The visit began at Launceston, where in the previous year pigs foraging for food in the castle moat had so weakened the walls that urgent repairs had been needed to prepare it for the Prince's arrival. He was met by John Kellygrew, who held his lands on condition that he act as the Prince's escort when in Cornwall, wearing a grey cloak. More than six hundred years later, in 1973, the present Prince of Wales received the feudal dues of his Cornish estates in a ceremony little changed since the Black

Representatives of the Duke of Cornwall's Cornish estates with their feudal dues at Launceston Castle in 1973, during the visit of the Prince of Wales.

Prince entered the town. Its mayor handed the Prince a hundred silver shillings and a pound of peppercorns. Stoke Climsland provided a salmon spear and the load of firewood which daily had to be brought to the castle when the Black Prince was in residence. From Truro came a bow, from the manor of Trevelga a pair of white gloves, whilst the manor of Elerky in Veryan contributed a pair of greyhounds. Such gifts may seem meaningless, but in the fourteenth century they were the expression of a political power that reached out into every hamlet in the Duchy. Like his successors, the Black Prince had the right to appoint Cornwall's high sheriff. From his Ducal bases in Lostwithiel and Restormel he controlled its government and courts, the election writs sending members to Parliament. No one was immune to his influence. Many of his Cornish tenants were little more than serfs, bound to the land at his will, and the last were only finally freed in the seventeenth century.

Cornwall's first Duke returned twice to his Duchy. But when he stepped ashore in Plymouth after sailing from France in 1371

The effigy of the Black Prince on his tomb in Canterbury Cathedral.

the long years of campaigning had taken their toll. Emaciated, worn thin by dysentery and a failing liver, he retired to Berkhamsted. Five years later, aged only forty-six, he died in his palace at Kennington. That autumn he was buried behind the high altar of Canterbury Cathedral, close to the shrine to St Thomas. On his tomb rests his armour-clad effigy, helmet open, hands joined in prayer, his dog at his feet; whilst above the canopy are reminders of what both made and destroyed him, his surcoat and gauntlets, shield and sword.

More than once over the next century the sword was to end the lives of Cornwall's dukes, or claimants to the title. Two were murdered and two killed in battle as Edward III's worst fears were realized and the struggle for the succession see-sawed to and fro. The Duchy fell apart as one duke after another rode roughshod over the safeguards built into the founding charter. Richard II granted the Cornish manors to his queen. Favourites and followers grew wealthy on estates only given to buy their loyalty. In 1421, Henry V endowed Syon Abbey with the Duchy manor of Isleworth in Middlesex, exchanging it for nineteen manors elsewhere, most of them in Somerset. The contest for the

lucrative stewardship of the Cornish estates led to a full-scale private war between rivals for the post.

The task of piecing the Duchy back together fell to Henry VII, and his eventual heir, Henry VIII. Estates were recovered, loyal officials given key appointments. But the national mood did little to help them. In 1497, high taxes inspired a Cornish rebellion that sent 15,000 rebels marching east beyond the Tamar towards inevitable defeat by Henry VII on the outskirts of London. Within months, a second uprising led by Perkin Warbeck again saw the West Country flare into rebellion. The cost of failure was high, with substantial fines being added to the taxes.

When Henry VIII became king in 1509 the lack of a son provided an excuse to appropriate the Duchy's income for himself. The sums were considerable, for the early sixteenth century marked a mining boom that helped increase the Duchy's contribution to the crown's revenue to almost five per cent. The new king was less scrupulous than his father. In 1538, Henry Courtenay, Marquis of Exeter and Lord Warden of the Stannaries, died on the scaffold on a trumped up charge of treason and his immense West Country estates were confiscated. The marquis's crime was to be Edward IV's grandson, and thus a possible claimant for the throne. To acquire the great Duchy manor of Wallingford, which Henry VIII wanted for himself, he exchanged it for the Courtenay's Cornish estates, and a group of much smaller manors, surrendered to the crown by the dissolved priories at Launceston and Tywardreath.

The Duchy's grip on the West Country tightened still further when the young Edward VI succeeded to the throne in 1547. By 1549 the lessons learnt by the Cornish fifty years earlier had apparently been forgotten. This time it was the enforced introduction of Cranmer's English prayer book that lit the spark. The Cornish rose in protest. The Protector, the Duke of Somerset, ordered the Duchy's income to be used to finance an army to enter Cornwall and put down the rebellion. It was a bitter contradiction. Rents paid by Cornishmen were paying the army sent to subdue them. The end result was the same. The rebels were annihilated, the gallows kept busy.

Like her father, Elizabeth I regarded the Duchy as a personal fiefdom whose revenues she could dispose of as she pleased.

Looking north up the Looe River past the towns of East and West Looe. After being confiscated from the Courtenay family in 1538, the two towns were granted to the Duchy by Henry VIII in exchange for the manor of Wallingford.

Throughout much of her reign, the Duchy was the single most important source of tin in Europe, and those able to divert a share of the profits into their own pockets grew rich as a result. The first to use tin as a stepping-stone was Sir William Godolphin, ancestor of a prime minister and founder of one of Cornwall's most influential dynasties. West of Helston, in the woods below the castellated hall built as proof of the

Godolphins' power, are the overgrown tin-workings on which their wealth was founded. In 1520 Sir William Godolphin was made Controller of the Coinage of Tin, a post he successfully defended with his sword when the controller appointed by Queen Mary entered Truro's Coinage Hall and demanded that the hammers used to stamp tin be handed over. Fifty years later, his nephew, Sir Francis, then the Duchy's Receiver General, was granted a lease on the Isles of Scilly, building Star Castle and forging a relationship between the Godolphins and the islands that lasted until well into the nineteenth century.

The other major beneficiary of the lack of a duke was cast in a very different mould. Courtier, poet, adventurer, warrior – no other figure so perfectly defines the contrasting aspects of the Elizabethan age as Sir Walter Raleigh. He was born a farmer's son near Budleigh Salterton in Devon, never renouncing his loyalty to the county. By 1587, the queen's affections had made him a knight, a member of parliament, Lord Lieutenant of Cornwall, a Vice Admiral, and Lord Warden of the Stannaries – the last of which most concerned the Duchy. A contemporary, complaining of his appointment and doubting his ability to control the mining community, described the tinners as 'so rough and mutinous a multitude'. By now, the original open-air tin-workings were beginning to be replaced by primitive ill-ventilated shaft mines, whose costs increased as they deepened. Conditions were appalling. 'No labourer whatsoever undergoes greater hazard . . . , nor in hard or coarse fare and diet doth equal him: bread, the brownest; cheese, the hardest; drink, the thinnest', began one account of mining. The price of tin fluctuated sharply, then fell, leading many into debt. Raleigh did what he could, introducing a series of reforms to the Stannaries that long outlived him. But his hold on power was fragile, and dependent on the queen. Elizabeth I showed scant interest in the Duchy, and began auctioning off manors to help replenish an exchequer drained by the costs of war. Her death brought the sales to a halt. Within months of James I becoming king in 1603, Raleigh had been stripped of his powers, accused of treason, and placed in the Tower. In 1616 he was led out onto the scaffold, leaving behind in a letter written to his wife on the night before his execution a request that he be buried beside his parents in

Sir Walter Raleigh (1552-1618), a miniature painted by Nicholas Hilliard in about 1585.

Exeter, and the most poignant of final farewells: 'I can say noe more, tyme and death call me away'.

Raleigh's election to Parliament hints at another of the ways by which the Duchy served its own interests. By the end of Elizabeth's reign, and despite having one of the lowest populations of any county, Cornwall returned the largest number of members of parliament. Tiny Looe, divided by the river, provided four of the forty-four. Sir Francis Drake sat as Member for Bossiney, which comprised the deserted ruins of Tintagel Castle and a single hamlet. When the seat was finally abolished by the 1832 Reform Act it contained twenty-five electors, only one of whom bothered to vote. The system was straightforward. The Duchy told the local gentry who to vote for, who in turn informed the electorate.

Powers of patronage such as these served the crown well when James I began the long-needed overhaul of the Duchy for his heir, Prince Henry. For nearly a century it had been either neglected or exploited. Annual revenues had fallen to below £5,000. The search for a Clerk to the Prince's Council produced not one applicant familiar with the privileges and rights which governed it. The prisoners in Lostwithiel gaol lay forgotten in a twelve by seventeen feet cell without windows or fireplace. Kennington Palace had been demolished. Lydford, Restormel and Berkhamsted castles were in ruins. There was nowhere within the Duchy for its dukes to make a home – an omission only finally righted when the Duchy bought Highgrove for the present Prince of Wales in 1980.

James I's first task was to recover the manors so profligately given away by his predecessor. The courts supported him, ruling that land granted to the Duchy by Act of Parliament could only be taken from it by later Acts. The death from fever of the king's heir, Prince Henry, when not yet eighteen in 1612, raised a second legal conundrum. The founding charter stated that only the monarch's eldest son could be Duke of Cornwall, thus excluding the new heir to the throne, Prince Charles (later Charles I). Once again the courts sided with the crown, setting a precedent allowing the Duchy and its revenues to be handed on to a younger brother.

Whatever Charles I's failings as king, and despite being only fifteen when he gained control of the Duchy in 1615, he proved a competent Duke of Cornwall. From his brother he inherited a half-timbered Council Chamber in Fleet Street. Later successively a tavern, waxworks, and barbers' shop, and now home to an exhibition celebrating Samuel Pepys, its jettied oriel window still survives, as does an ornate plaster ceiling decorated with the Prince of Wales feathers. Here Charles gathered round him a Prince's Council of skilled administrators that included Sir Francis Bacon, and, as Master of the Prince's Game, the uncle of the man who eventually drove him from the throne, Oliver Cromwell. Revenues rose. The cartographer John Norden spent six years surveying the Duchy, mapping and valuing estates. Rents were reviewed before new leases issued. As was traditional in the West Country, these leases were usually for a number of lives rather than years. Norden thought that 'the healthsome ayre wherein they live' convinced most tenants that a long life was a safer bet than a fixed number of years, but extra lives could be bought in such tenancies, often extending them for centuries. The right to buy all tin as it came on the market

RIGHT *Charles I (1600-1649), engraved from a portrait when still Prince of Wales and Duke of Cornwall.*

BELOW *The half-timbered exterior of Prince Henry's Council Chamber in Fleet Street, built in 1610.*

was also leased, and profitably, to a group that included the fledgeling East India Company. These reforms were not always popular. When Charles first became duke, all existing leases had been declared void. Parliament disapproved, passing an Act guaranteeing existing tenancies when one duke succeeded another.

High-handedness was balanced by paternalism. Norden might grumble that tenants were born 'litigious', inclined to lay 'quarrels for small causes', but they were allowed to lodge any complaints directly to the Prince's Council – and did so. Unusually, instead of confiscating the entire estate of a Cornishman convicted of manslaughter, only a percentage was taken, the rest distributed to his children. The Cornish genius for ignoring what does not suit them also helped their cause. Rents might be due, promises made, but neither guaranteed payment. Calstock's reeve endlessly demanded its tenants pay-up, but few did, and some rents were still unpaid when twelve years in arrears.

West Sedge Moor on the southern side of the Somerset Levels.

One document to have survived from the period is the inventory of a widow, Mary Pytte, who died in 1640 in a cottage leased from the Duchy near Isle Abbots, on the edge of the Somerset Levels. The cob cottage, with its smoke-blackened walls, was originally open to the ceiling, and the upper floor had only been added shortly after the defeat of the Armada. Then, as now, the badly-drained Levels provided good pasture for cattle, and Mary Pytte's six cows grazed the open fields she shared with other smallholders. In the kitchen was her cheese-making equipment – a press, vats, perforated bowls – whilst upstairs, where she kept her bacon and cider, were five hundredweight cheeses not yet mature enough to be sold. Outside in the yard, were the pair of pigs she fattened on the surplus whey.

Mary Pytte's possessions were valued at £79, and although the inventory is a far cry from the world of her landlord it vividly evokes the preoccupations of a seventeenth century yeoman farmer's wife of modest means. Prince Charles probably knew nothing of Mary Pytte's existence, for the Duchy then had many thousands of tenants, but by deliberately creating a centralized London-based bureaucracy he was unwittingly distancing the Duchy from those it sought to rule. In time, this remoteness would place the relationship between landlord and tenant under considerable strain. Few seventeenth or eighteenth century dukes ever visited their Duchy, or took much interest in it. Of course they were happy to spend its revenues, which they did with gusto, but real power gradually passed from the dukes to their officials.

Not far from Isle Abbots, also on the rim of the Levels, lies Falconer's Farm, a Duchy holding since the reign of Henry V, and today the home of Simon Peach and his family. The honey-coloured Ham Hill stone farmhouse with its mullioned windows sits comfortably amidst cider orchards and small high-hedged fields, evoking a way of life little changed over the centuries, and one which Mary Pytte would still find familiar. The 300 acre farm is the traditional Somerset mix of arable, dairy, beef herd, and cider apples. Alongside its boundary with the River Yeo lie the old common meadows, Milton Mead and Milton Leaze, where the different strips, or 'doles', remain divided by ancient dole stones marking the land to which each villager was entitled.

Three generations of the Peach family, tenants of Falconer's Farm, Milton Falconbridge, on the edge of the Somerset Levels.

LEFT *Bob Peach in the meadows alongside the River Yeo. Visible amid the grass are the dole stones marking the land to which each villager was entitled when the field was common meadow.*

RIGHT *Bob Peach outside the farmhouse.*

BELOW *Simon and Judith Peach, together with their son Robert, gathering fallen cider apples in the orchards.*

Some strips are as narrow as fifteen feet, and although time has sucked some of the stones deep into the moor, many stand two feet high, with the initials of those who farmed the strips carved on one face. Both dole stones and open meadows are rare survivals from the days before enclosure. To preserve their ley of traditional grasses, the meadows can't be sprayed, but they provide Simon Peach with valuable spring grazing for his cattle, after which they are cut for hay. Closer to the farm four acres of cider orchards fill fields still contoured by the ridges and furrows formed when they first were ploughed. Under old Duchy tenancies, existing orchards had to be maintained, but as cider went out of fashion the arrangement lapsed and many were grubbed out. In 1980 Simon Peach and his father, Bob, sensed that the wheel was about to turn and began replanting, mixing varieties to help pollination. To walk the rows as Simon calls out the names – Slack-me-Girdle, Brown Snout, Tom Putt, Chisel Jerseys – is almost to taste the bitter-sweet flavour of farmhouse 'scrumpy'. His prediction has proved correct. Although vulnerable to late frost, the orchards are now yielding about five tons of apples to the acre, providing a useful income from less productive land that can also be grazed by his young stock.

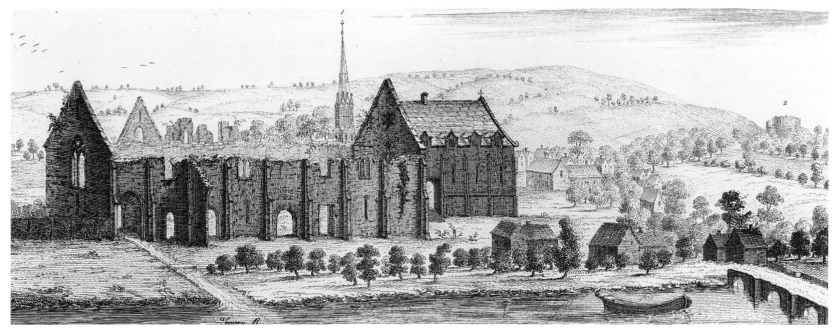

The remains of the Duchy Palace at Lostwithiel, engraved by Samuel and Nathaniel Buck, 1734.

In 1642 Charles I's refusal to bend to Parliament's will resulted in Civil War. For the next few years the Duchy's fortunes ebbed and flowed in time to those of the king. Cornwall suffered the worst, particularly after 1645 when the king granted the Duchy to his heir, later Charles II, and sent him west in hope of uniting the West Country to the Royalist cause. Tin production doubled to pay for munitions, unpaid rents were hastily gathered. But the end result was the same. A year later, the young duke boarded a ship for the Isles of Scilly, from where he finally fled to France, and in 1649 Parliament ordered the entire Duchy to be broken up and sold.

Prior to dismantling its newest windfall, Parliament commissioned a survey to assess its value. The survey survives, providing a valuable snapshot of the health of the Duchy approximately halfway through its history. The results were unimpressive. Most Cornish tenants held their land on a rolling seven year lease, which effectively made them freeholders. Elsewhere tenancies ranged from thirty-one to ninety-nine years, and many had been sub-let at substantially higher rents. The great medieval

fortresses once so visible a statement of the Duchy's prestige were all in ruins. Launceston Castle had been stripped of its lead during the Civil War. The gardens and orchards planted round Rougemont Castle in the belief that its military days were over had been uprooted. Most to be regretted is the Duchy Palace at Lostwithiel, which today survives as a buttressed fragment tacked on to the Masonic Hall: the gable wall still carries a weatherworn stone shield on which the fifteen 'byzants' of the Duchy's coat-of-arms can just be counted.

The main beneficiaries of Parliament's sale of the Duchy were local gentry sympathetic to Parliament and soldiers in Cromwell's army with money to spend. The enjoyment of their new estates was short-lived. Following the Restoration in 1660, and Charles II's triumphant accession to the throne, all sales of freeholds were declared void and converted into leases. The Duchy was pieced back together. Perhaps surprisingly, it proved more resilient than might be expected, and when next assessed proved only slightly smaller than at the start of the Civil War. Yet something had been lost, and forever. The Duchy's self-confidence had been badly bruised; never again would it enjoy its traditional influence and power.

By the date of the Restoration the Duchy's offices had moved from Fleet Street into Somerset House. As well as a Council Chamber, auditor and surveyor's offices, there was a wine cellar – hinting, perhaps, at a new more ebullient mood. But in reality little changed until the advent of the Hanoverians in 1714, who provided the Duchy with all three of its eighteenth century dukes. George, Prince of Wales (later George II), Prince Frederick, and Prince George Augustus (later Prince Regent and George IV), governed their Duchy through a period that saw it reach the lowest point in its fortunes. They quarrelled incessantly. Scandal surrounded them. The second, 'Poor Fred', enjoyed an income from the Duchy that by the 1730s was in excess of £30,000 – an enormous sum for those days. Part paid for Kew and Cliveden, yet he was permanently in debt. His 'chief passion', wrote Horace Walpole, 'was women, but, like all his race, beauty was not a necessary ingredient'. The Prince Regent stayed firmly in Carlton House, or his new seaside Pavilion in Brighton. Although he encouraged others to initiate various schemes, he failed to shape policies capable of leading the Duchy forward – a state that continued during the brief reign of his brother, William IV, from 1830 to 1837, and was made worse by the lack of an heir.

In the 1780s the Prince's Council commissioned William Simpson to survey the Duchy's holdings and assess their values. Simpson was an 'improver', an advocate of new roads and fertilisers. But nothing came of his recommendations, and in 1798 the Duchy's long-term prospects were significantly worsened by the passage through Parliament of the Land Tax Act to help meet the costs of fighting Napoleon. Although subject to the tax, the Duchy was permitted to redeem it by selling land and investing the proceeds in government stock. The impact was immediate. By the turn of the century estates in Berkshire, Cornwall, Leicestershire, Lincolnshire and Sussex had been sold, often at a knock-down price, many of them part of the Duchy since its creation.

Elsewhere, corruption and neglect were in the ascendant. Although output from the Dartmoor and Cornish tin mines was

ABOVE *Frederick, Prince of Wales (1707-1751).*

RIGHT *George, Prince of Wales, later Prince Regent and George IV (1762-1830).*

rising, coinage dues were falling rapidly. Stewards policed their own tenancies. Ramshackle land laws and medieval systems of tenure allowed farms to be endlessly divided, leading to absentee lease-holders demanding exorbitant rents for portions of land so minute a tenant in Stoke Climsland held less than five square yards. Others profited by the reverse process: one Cornish farmer happily explained the growth of his farm from 48 to 200 acres as due to a grandfather who was 'uncommon industrious. He often hedged by lantern and candle'.

One of many to take advantage of the Duchy's shortcomings was the shadowy figure of Benjamin Tucker, who rose from obscurity as a ship's purser to become Second Secretary of the Admiralty. In 1807 Tucker obtained a ninety year lease of Trematon Castle, which brought with it rights over much of the River Tamar. The following year he was appointed Surveyor General to the entire Duchy, a post given firmer footings by the gift of a Cornish silver snuff-box to the Prince Regent. Once a member of the Prince's Council, Tucker used his influence to help his sons. One became an admiral, another Deputy Receiver,

Trematon Castle, with the Regency villa built by Benjamin Tucker in its grounds. Antony Passage curls round to the left, whilst the entrance to the Lynher River from the Tamar is on the right.

a third his Deputy Surveyor. Other privileges were gradually harvested, lining his pockets still further. The Castle had long been empty. Drake had used its keep as a temporary store for Spanish plunder, but a brutal Civil War siege during which Royalist fingers were broken to remove their owners' rings had left it a ruin. After first demolishing yet more of the walls to improve his view of the Tamar, Tucker built a Regency villa in the Castle grounds. Many years later, when Queen Victoria first visited the West Country with Prince Albert, she is reputed to have glanced up at it from the river and remarked, 'it all belongs to Bertie'. Edward VII did indeed inherit Trematon when the Tuckers' lease expired, and both Castle and villa remain Duchy property – leading most recently to two stonemasons spending fifteen years repairing and repointing its walls.

Three years after Benjamin Tucker's death the great Reform Act of 1832 swept away another of the Duchy's ancient sources of influence. The 'rotten' and 'pocket' boroughs that made up many of the forty-four Parliamentary seats in Cornwall were abolished, and the number of Cornish M.P.s reduced to twelve. In the new age of industrial capitalism the Duchy was increasingly perceived as the symbol of a feudal past, an out-of-date brake on the forces of progress. Nowhere were the lines more sharply drawn than over the coinage dues paid it by the tin industry. The new breed of hard-headed mine-owners saw such payments as a means of clinging on to rights and customs that were both ill-defined and obsolete. The radical *West Briton* newspaper launched itself into the fray, challenging the right of the Duchy to 'sacrifice' the tin mines 'in order to supply a revenue for the Heir Apparent'.

The Duchy was most vulnerable over claims to mineral royalties on estates it had sold. In 1817 it leased these dues to a collector whose high-handed methods caused some mines to shut down. Ten years later a long-running dispute over copper royalties in one Cornish mine led to a series of complicated legal cases that ultimately returned ownership of the mine to the Duchy. But the costs were prodigious, lawyers its main beneficiaries. The documents used as evidence in one case alone weighed three-quarters of a ton. A group of Cornish witnesses, once certain the Duchy was paying their expenses, consumed 370 grogs and 50 bottles of wine in a single day.

In 1838 the Duchy bowed to the pressure for change. Although it continued to receive both royalties and rents on mines it owned, it agreed to surrender its Stannary duties on the coinage of tin in return for an annual payment from the Treasury. The amount was based on the average yield of coinage dues in the previous ten years, saddling the Duchy with a fixed sum that took no account of the massive increase in tin and copper production later in the century. The sum agreed was approximately £16,000, nearly half its total revenue. A further Act of 1838 established a second precedent by which the Duchy was legally obliged to present annual accounts to Parliament. For the first time in five hundred years it could be held publicly responsible for the management of its affairs.

Against this background, with the Duchy weakened and its ancient traditions under threat, a new recruit took his seat at the Council table. In 1840, the year of his marriage, Prince Albert was twenty-one, the same age as his bride. A painting of their

A detail from 'The Marriage of Queen Victoria', 10 February, 1840, by Sir George Hayter.

wedding in the Chapel Royal, St James's Palace, shows the young Queen Victoria gazing admiringly at a tall elegantly-dressed figure with an open intelligent face. No other person so perfectly sums up the aspirations of the age. The Queen might complain of his 'over love of business', but there can be little doubt of her husband's abilities. Blessed with energy, interested in and knowledgeable about architecture, agriculture, engineering, science and the arts, Prince Albert brought to the Duchy an eagerness for reform and determination to see it efficiently managed unequalled by any of his predecessors.

Understandably, Queen Victoria was content to leave the management of the Duchy to her husband. Decisions might be made collectively by the Prince's Council, but following Prince Albert's appointment as Lord Warden of the Stannaries it was he who shaped its policies. The guiding principles were first suggested by an old family friend, Baron Stockmar, who in a letter to the Prince wrote: 'avoid going too deep into details, which will only bewilder you. The fundamental principle to

31

which you have to hold fast is that the Duchy is altogether a private affair with which neither the Government nor its ministers have, or ought to have, anything to do'.

But the 'private affair' was now publicly accountable, and if the Duchy was to survive it needed first to be put in order. His first problem was a domestic one. The Queen's governess, Baroness Lehzen, used her influence to try and acquire the Duchy's revenues for herself. Albert despatched her to Germany, then set to work. Within the next few years the fees paid office-holders were abolished and the Duchy granted powers to buy and sell land. Most significantly of all, the complex systems of land tenure were at last simplified in favour of standard annual agreements that allowed rents to be raised and copyhold tenants and absentee landlords bought out.

These were radical reforms. As overheads fell, so income from farmland and the increasingly urban estate in Kennington increased, reducing the Duchy's dependency on revenues from mining. Money could finally be ploughed back into improvements. Cottages were renovated, land levelled, cowsheds built, bringing the Prince's Council into much closer contact with tenants and gradually giving them a voice in their own affairs. Instead of allowing officials to acquire a number of offices as a means of bolstering their fees, salaried staff with specific skills were taken on. The first Land Steward was appointed, who from an office in Lostwithiel collected rents, dealt with day-to-day matters, and provided the Prince's Council with regular reports on the Duchy's health. The need for someone to advise the Council led to the appointment of a barrister, John Gardiner, as the Duchy's first Secretary, a post he combined with Vice Warden of the Stannaries and steward of the few surviving manorial courts.

Income rose accordingly; from £38,000 in 1840 to nearly £69,000 by 1860, of which £25,000 remained when all expenses had been paid. At least part of this went into the building of Osborne House on the Isle of Wight, but as surpluses accumulated a percentage was invested in the City. In twenty years the Duchy had been redefined. Power had dwindled to influence. Its constitutional and political importance belonged to the past, and it was essentially a commercial organization.

The Council Chamber, 10 Buckingham Gate.

To meet its new needs, the Duchy moved offices. Its new home was on the corner of Buckingham Gate, facing Buckingham Palace, in a building whose external façade is typically neo-Classical but whose interior conceals two comfortably spacious rooms, the Secretary's office and the Prince's Council Chamber. Its architect was Sir James Pennethorne, to whom we owe both Battersea Park and the present appearance of Regent Street, and 10 Buckingham Gate has remained the Duchy's headquarters to this day.

In 1859 Prince Albert travelled to Plymouth by train to open Brunel's new bridge over the Tamar. Carrying the broad-gauge

The opening of the Royal Albert Bridge over the River Tamar by Prince Albert in 1859.

tracks of the Great Western Railway high over the river on narrow piers, it was just the sort of large-scale engineering project the Prince most applauded. The central pier stands on river-bed owned by the Duchy, for which Brunel negotiated a fixed annual rent of £25 – the sum still paid today. Perhaps the rent did not matter, for the opening of the Royal Albert Bridge brought Buckingham Gate within a day's journey of the Duchy's Cornish estate. Equally importantly, it opened up new markets for West Country mines, helping animate a whirlwind spiral of boom and bust that only finally exhausted itself early in the twentieth century. The catalysts were the wider availability of

gunpowder, and the skill of engineers like Richard Trevithick, whose powerful steam-driven beam engine allowed water to be pumped from much greater depths. By the 1850s 300 mines were in production in Cornwall alone, filling every horizon with the now derelict carcasses of the buildings that housed the engines.

These were heady days. In 1836 copper was struck on the flank of Caradon Hill, north of Liskeard on the edge of Bodmin Moor. Over the next thirty years, on an initial capital of £637, South Caradon paid its investors £316,000 in dividends. Miners and their families poured into the area. The hamlets round the village of Minions were transformed into a Klondyke shanty town as

TOP *Dolcoath Copper Mine, near Camborne, in 1831.*

ABOVE *The Prince and Princess of Wales in the Prince of Wales shaft of the Phoenix United Mine during their visit to the mine in 1909.*

OPPOSITE PAGE *The Prince of Wales engine house, once part of the Phoenix United Mine.*

new mines were opened and a railway built linking it with the small port of Looe. One such mine was Phoenix United, a maze of workings that stretched for a mile beneath land owned by the Duchy near Minions. Like all those on Duchy land, the mine paid an annual rent and a royalty based on the value of its output, a total of about £1,500 in its most productive years.

Any lingering nostalgia for mining's past is misplaced. Those employed in Phoenix United included children, who spent their days washing and dressing the ore in sheds on the surface. The Prince of Wales shaft reached 1,200 feet. Off it ran a honeycomb of horizontal galleries that led to the lodes being mined. Temperatures below were well over a hundred, and a miner could easily lose six pounds in weight on a single shift. Death from consumption and other chest diseases was commonplace. The system by which only twelve months' wages were paid for a calendar year led to strikes and lockouts, whilst pay days were followed by 'Maze Mondays' – so named because a weekend spent in the local gin houses, brothels and beer shops left many nursing hangovers.

In 1897 Phoenix United closed, to be reborn in 1907 under new ownership on a thirty-one year lease from the Duchy at an annual rent of £50 and a royalty of one-thirtieth. Two years later, by which time £80,000 had been swallowed in pumping costs, the Prince and Princess of Wales (late George V and Queen Mary) visited the mine. The royal visit to what even then was the last mine operating in the area only delayed the inevitable. Like many mines, the Phoenix United rarely showed a profit, and in 1914 the great boilers in Houseman's and the Prince of Wales' engine houses were finally shut down.

In recent years, the Duchy of Cornwall has sold both engine houses to Caradon District Council as part of a scheme to attract low impact tourism to the area round the Minions by awakening interest in its archaeological and industrial past. Houseman's Engine House has been converted into a display centre, cattle grids and car parks have been provided. Land owned by the Duchy has been brought into the project, such as the nearby Cheesewring Quarry. In its heyday the quarry had provided granite for Tower Bridge, but the gullies and overhangs on its face now test the skills of visiting rock climbers. In summer,

botanists scramble through the undergrowth in search of the rare copper-tolerant mosses and lichens that grow in the shelter of the old mine workings, some of which are fluorescent. Within sight of the quarry is an unremarkable mound that could easily be mistaken for overgrown mine waste. Its name is Rillaton barrow, where in 1837 miners unearthed a Bronze Age burial tomb containing a skeleton, glass beads, a bronze dagger, and a small gold cup. The burial of a gold cup on the windswept fringes of Bodmin Moor hints at the area's archaeological importance. On the nearby skyline stone banks surround the raised platforms on which the first settlers built their huts. Rows of stones form mysterious alignments with barrows, avenues and three stone circles known as the Hurlers. Because the gold cup had been found on land belonging to the Duchy, it was sent to William IV. After his death it disappeared into the museum at Osborne, only resurfacing when George V chose it as a stud box for his dressing table. Today, the Rillaton Gold Cup is one of the treasures of the British Museum.

ABOVE LEFT *The Cheesewring Quarry, with the precarious pile of stones after which it is named visible on the skyline to the left. The carvings on the stone in the foreground were the work of Daniel Gumb, an eccentric 18th century stonecutter, who made his home in a cave on the moor, studying the stars by night and incising geometrical theories onto suitable rocks.*

ABOVE *The Rillaton gold cup.*

OPPOSITE PAGE *Disused engine houses on the Crowns, near Botallack Head in north Cornwall.*

The scars made by the mines have now healed. The last of the Dartmoor mines, the Golden Dagger, closed in the 1930s. A second engine house on Duchy land near Tintagel has been handed over to the North Cornwall Heritage Coast Service. Its only income from the industry today comes from a lease allowing the Poldark Mine near Helston to let visitors inspect the old underground workings, and the occasional hopeful prospector wishing to sift over ore-bearing rocks on a beach between tides, armed with a sack.

In November 1861, two years after opening the Royal Albert Bridge, Prince Albert took to his bed complaining of fever. A month later he was dead: he was forty-two. Disraeli's salute to 'this German prince who has governed England for twenty-one years with a wisdom and energy such as none of our Kings have ever shown' could as easily be applied to the Duchy of Cornwall. Of course he had faults. He failed to put back into the mining community even a fraction of what the Duchy took out, by way of welfare or encouraging higher wages. He also refused to allow Prince Edward (later Edward VII) to play any part in Duchy affairs, despite its providing his income. But on the credit side he had single-handedly steered the Duchy into calmer more profitable waters, creating an administration and management he would still find recognizable today. Shortly after his death, in 1863, the reforms he had set in motion were enshrined in the Duchy of Cornwall Management Act, an act that was to govern the Duchy's affairs for more than a century.

The years through which Prince Edward and his heir (later George V) chaired the meetings of the Prince's Council were marked by recession. Foreign imports undercut tin and copper prices, leading many miners to seek their fortunes abroad. The birth of refrigeration put Argentinian beef and New Zealand lamb on English butchers' counters. Wheat prices collapsed as the limitless prairies of North America were ploughed up and planted. In response, farm rents were left static, but the Duchy's revenues continued to climb as Kennington's streets filled with row upon row of cheap terraced housing. Although the Management Act of 1863 was later seen as a constraint on the Duchy's freedom to institute change, it did provide a legal framework to the ways in which it operated. Land began to be bought: a tentative 74 acres in Somerset, then 800 in Dorset, finally the 2,275 acre Whiteford estate built up near Stoke Climsland by Sir John Call, a poor Cornishman whose descendants squandered the fortune he had made in India.

All of the land bought in the late nineteenth century was in the West Country, strengthening the Duchy's traditional links with the region. But its duke was happiest in Norfolk, at Sandringham, and played little part in the running of his duchy. The turf, shooting, and a succession of mistresses were his main preoccupations, weaknesses that endeared him to most of his subjects. He was also extravagant, and in the 1880s the foreshore rights at Torquay, Paignton and Brixham were gradually sold, depriving his successors of potentially lucrative revenues.

A further source of income that reached its peak in this period was the North Somerset coalfield, where the Duchy had owned land since the fifteenth century. The Somerset coalfield was small, rural, and primitive – a backwater where miners worked thin fault-ridden seams in conditions that would have appalled miners from other areas. The coalfield was centred round Radstock and Midsomer Norton, where in 1633 Richard Mogg, the Duchy bailiff at Farrington Gurney, applied for a license to explore for coal beneath the estate. A shaft was sunk, and soon closed, and though his heirs tried to keep the mine going it didn't really start paying the Duchy a worthwhile royalty until the 1780s, the decade marking the real beginning of Somerset mining.

By the middle of the nineteenth century royalties from the four mines on Duchy land were running at about £2,000 a year, or approximately 6d a ton. Typical was Clandown, which opened in 1801 and whose shaft reached 1,200 feet before striking coal. The narrow seams were rarely wider than a man, so that to work

LEFT *A rare view of Clandown Colliery in 1908. The Colliery stood on Duchy land near Midsomer Norton. It opened in 1801 and closed in 1929.*

RIGHT *The magnificent Dundas Aqueduct south of Bath. The aqueduct was designed by John Rennie and built between 1796 and 1799 to carry the Kennet and Avon Canal over the River Avon. In the foreground on the right is the junction with the Somerset Coal Canal, built partly over Duchy land to transport coal from the Somerset Coalfield.*

them miners lay flat on their backs and swung small picks overhead at the face. The coal was shifted by 'guss and crook', by which carting boys crawled on all fours with a chain between their legs attached to a coal-laden sledge. Faced with such conditions, it is easy to understand the horror of the miner who, after being found drunk in a lane, was carried underground as a joke, and on finally sobering up believed himself in hell.

Despite the Somerset mining song promising 'The future's bright before us, if firmly we press on', the coalfield began losing money. From early in the 1920s one pit after the next was forced to close. The then Prince of Wales (later Edward VIII), did what he could to keep the coalfield alive, waiving all royalties and rent when a group of unemployed miners formed a small co-operative called the Marsh Lane Colliery. The colliery sold its daily production of eight or nine tons at the pithead, and its two delivery lorries were locally a familiar sight until 1949 when the seam became too narrow to work.

To show his support for the mine, the Prince of Wales went underground in a coal tub, afterwards washing with soap and towels provided by a miner's wife. Such informality and obvious concern for the plight of the unemployed would have once been unthinkable. For although Edward VII's accession to the throne in 1901 blew away the cobwebs of the Victorian age, it was his grandson who really captured the changing mood of the new century.

Prince Edward became Duke of Cornwall at the age of fifteen in 1910 when his father, George V, followed Edward VII on to the throne. The Duchy Secretary was by then Sir Walter Peacock, another barrister, but a perhaps more significant appointment was that of Lord Revelstoke, senior partner in Baring Brothers, his family's merchant bank, as Duchy Receiver General, the ancient office controlling its finances. By 1910 the Duchy's income stood at over £160,000, sufficient for the two men to accumulate a surplus of £400,000 by the time the Prince reached twenty-one and had the right to his inheritance. In 1921, citing higher repair bills and personal expenses, the Prince persuaded the Treasury to exempt the Duchy from income tax, replacing it with a voluntary contribution. Such were the savings, the Prince loaned George V £90,000 to buy additional land at Sandringham, a debt which he finally abandoned any hope of collecting shortly before the King's death.

In the summer of 1914 Prince Edward opened a new church and toured working class housing on Duchy land in Kennington. It was his first solo performance as Duke. Admitting his ignorance of conditions on the estate, he afterwards resolved to do all he could to improve the 'comfort and happiness' of his tenants. The words were carefully chosen. By publicly associating himself with the poor and unemployed, he set the tone for policies that dominated the Duchy for the next twenty years, and remain central to those followed by the present Prince of Wales. Prince Edward was young. He had stamina, enthusiasm and boundless goodwill. But he was easily bored and lacked concentration, which in turn meant that much of the work of running the Duchy was delegated to the Land Stewards, reducing the importance of the Prince's Council.

Despite his faults, Prince Edward gave the Duchy a human face. To symbolize his dislike of pomp, the only flag flown from Fort Belvedere, his home on the edge of Windsor Great Park, was that of the Duchy. As king, he walked unescorted to its offices from Buckingham Palace, causing one outraged M.P. to demand he cease doing 'this sort of thing'. He made regular visits to Duchy farms, paying particular attention to rural housing and ways of creating employment. Above all, he genuinely cared for his tenants, inspiring an affection and loyalty that survived the Abdication.

In 1912, when the Prince was eighteen, a young architect called Albert Richardson was appointed to design new farmhouses and cottages for the Duchy. Over the next twenty years he built terraced housing in Dorchester and Princetown, as well as numerous brick and slate-roofed farmhouses. Modest substance combined with lack of pretension makes them easily recognizable, and many are still home to Duchy farmers and their families. These same qualities are also evident in Richardson's most ambitious project for the Duchy, the transforming of Sir John Call's granite mansion at Stoke Climsland into the Duchy Home Farm. After incorporating what he could into the new house, the rest was pulled down, its stucco dispersed to other Duchy farmhouses, and its Adam fireplace despatched to

Buckingham Gate to help warm the Council Chamber. An avenue of sweet chestnuts leads to the farm and its range of buildings, which Richardson topped with a bell-cote and a crest bearing the Prince of Wales' feathers. It is now called Duchy College, and though still owned by the Duchy is let as a county agricultural college to Cornwall County Council.

The future Edward VIII spent what time he could at Stoke Climsland, involving himself in improving the beef herd, and forming a close friendship with its rector, Canon Martin Andrews. Their friendship grew out of a shared concern for the unemployed, and led to the Duchy funding market gardens near the village as a means of creating jobs. A second Cornish farm

TOP *The old Duchy Home Farm, Stoke Climsland, now part of Duchy College, and all that remains of Sir John Call's original mansion.*

BOTTOM *Some of the buildings designed by Albert Richardson for George V for the Duchy Home Farm at Stoke Climsland.*

RIGHT *The Prince of Wales inspecting his prize bull, Coombehead Monarch, at the Duchy Home Farm, Stoke Climsland, in 1933.*

Clearing rubble from 10 Buckingham Gate following bomb damage during a German raid in May 1941.

was turned into a poultry enterprise. On the Isles of Scilly, an experimental station was opened to research better methods of growing bulbs. Elsewhere, land was leased to County Councils to provide smallholdings for young farmers eager to gain a foothold on the farming ladder. At Tor Royal, on Dartmoor, thirty men were given work in a stud set up to winter the Prince's polo ponies, school his hunters, and train the horses he rode during such ceremonies as Trooping the Colour.

Following the Abdication, the lack of a male heir meant that responsibility for the Duchy passed to George VI, and accompanied by Queen Elizabeth the new King visited both Devon and Cornwall in 1937. The outbreak of war placed burdens on the King that made it harder to take an active role in the daily management of the Duchy, a task made temporarily impossible when a German raid over London in 1941 led to Buckingham Gate being bombed and the collapse of part of the building. Yet despite the uncertainty, the King embarked on a series of purchases that by his death in 1952 had increased the size of the Duchy by nearly 20,000 acres. Most of the new land was in Cornwall, but the largest was the 4,800 acre Newton Park Estate, west of Bath, which was sold to the Duchy in 1941 following the death of Lord Temple.

On a damp November evening in 1948 tenants the length and breadth of the Duchy – from those gathered in a remote whitewashed cottage on the Isles of Scilly, to the London cabbie hurrying home to his Kennington terrace – tuned in their wirelesses to news that many had been waiting for, Princess Elizabeth had given birth to a son. On her accession, the Duchy of Cornwall would have a new Duke, the first since the birth of Edward VIII more than half-a-century earlier. Twenty-one years later, in November 1969, Prince Charles entered Buckingham Gate, climbed the stairs sweeping up to the first floor, and sat down at one end of the mahogany table in the Prince's Council Chamber. Now that he was twenty-one he was entitled to take an active role in the Duchy that provided his income. Behind him, above the fireplace, lay the whole weight of its history in the form of a plasterwork cartouche embellished with the fifteen coins given its coat-of-arms by Edward III. Ahead lay his inheritance.

Shaping the Present

When Prince Charles chaired his first meeting of the Prince's Council he had only a vague understanding of the institution from which he drew his income. It was November 1969, exactly a week after his twenty-first birthday. He was in his last year at Cambridge. Though the pageantry of his investiture as Prince of Wales at Caernarvon Castle earlier in the year had taught him much about what others expected of him he had yet to find a focus for his energy and talents. The Duchy, it was hoped, might well hold the key. Ranged round the table were the eight Council members appointed by his mother, the Queen, one of whom, Sir Patrick Kingsley, had been its Secretary for ten years – a role he combined with that of Keeper of the Records. Others bore similar titles, which though reflecting the antiquity of their offices imparted an almost Ruritanian air to the gathering. There was the Lord Warden of the Stannaries, the Receiver and Attorney Generals. More down-to-earth were the four Land Stewards, each representing the areas where the Duchy was traditionally strongest – Kennington, the Isles of Scilly, Cornwall and the West Country.

The Prince's first task was to exercise a right enjoyed by successive dukes since the Duchy's medieval foundation, the appointment of a new High Sheriff of Cornwall. The choice was straightforward, the discussion brief. But the next item was less easy to hurry. The Plymouth and South Devon Water Authorities wanted to build a reservoir on land owned by the Duchy on Dartmoor. Privately the Council objected. Publicly it had to stay silent. Any hint of criticism might imply the Prince interfering in government policy. And so it went on. Though much was a recital of tenants retiring and farms in need of improvement other items required more delicate handling. Elsewhere on Dartmoor, the Ministry of Defence lease of land for a firing range was due for renewal. Some houses in Kennington had been demolished to make way for redevelopment. A petition had been received insisting on the freedom to put down moorings on a Cornish river.

As Prince Charles became more familiar with his inheritance, it gradually became clear that though adept at side-stepping controversy the Duchy was in need of modernizing. Its main problems were financial. When the Queen came to the throne following the death of George VI it had been agreed with the Treasury that a ninth of the Duchy's income was to be made available for the Prince's maintenance, a figure amended to £30,000 a year between his eighteenth and twenty-first birthdays. The balance was to be paid to the Treasury and offset against the cost of the Civil List. Throughout the 1950s and 60s the Duchy marked time. There was little incentive for reform. Prince Charles was still only a boy, and the lack of a Duke of Cornwall actively involved in the Duchy's management meant Sir Patrick Kingsley's main responsibility lay in preserving its health until the Prince came of age. He did so in the courteous unassuming style appropriate to the period. For post-war Britain was very different from today. Duchy affairs were conducted at an unhurried gentlemanly pace, which only began to quicken when the election of the Labour government under Harold Wilson in 1964 made the future less certain.

Although over 12,000 acres were bought by the Duchy between

The Prince of Wales chatting to tenants in Kennington during a visit in 1971.

the end of the war and 1969, Duchy rents had lagged behind others. The need for essential repairs combined with post-war rent controls turned Kennington into a drain on capital: Surrey County Cricket Club paid £10 a year in rent for the Oval. The lack of a firm hand at the helm meant that little attention was paid to the larger needs of the Duchy as a whole. Each Land Steward ran his district as a semi-autonomous fiefdom, one visiting his tenants in a chauffeur-driven car. The only occasion they met as a group was when once a year they were treated to dinner in London with their wives and given tickets for the theatre. Every district had cottages without bathrooms, tenants paying rents even lower than that of the Oval.

Now that the Prince was twenty-one, all the Duchy's net profits were legally his. Its annual surplus stood at just under £250,000, half of which he agreed to pay to the Treasury in lieu of income tax, then ninety per cent at the top rate. Because he received nothing from the Civil List, the Prince relied entirely on the

Duchy. Though it was clear that its income was insufficient to meet the Prince's growing expenses nothing much was done until the appointment of Anthony Gray as Secretary in 1972. Tony Gray came to Buckingham Gate from Christ Church, Oxford, where as treasurer he had reorganized its estates. His liking for a leisurely lunch concealed a sharp intelligence that quickly perceived that the long-term future of the Duchy needed to be underpinned by increasing its revenues and adding to its capital. Rents gradually rose. The Duchy's investments were spread more widely to lessen its dependency on land. Reports were commissioned to suggest assets that could be sold and estates in need of improvement. As changes in farming techniques and increasingly efficient machinery reduced the numbers needed to work the land, so surplus farm cottages were sold and smaller holdings amalgamated. Younger faces joined the Duchy, the boundaries of the districts were redrawn.

Many of these innovations were initiated by the team of professional advisers Tony Gray gathered around him. If as Secretary he was its dominant influence, he was content to leave much of the day-to-day work of running the Duchy to others. Conversations with those long familiar with the Duchy summon up names from this period in its past, but to whom its present owes much. For many years his Deputy was Michael Ruffer, as eccentric as he was loyal, who when crossing Buckingham Gate halted the oncoming traffic with an outstretched umbrella in the belief that servants of the crown took precedence. As Lord Warden of the Stannaries, the then Earl Waldegrave alerted his fellow members of the Prince's Council to the need for reform. A more recent Lord Warden, Lord Ashburton, a member of the Baring family, first became involved with the Duchy as its Receiver General in the 1970s, bringing a sharper focus to its financial affairs. Jack Hickish and John Hitchings, Land Stewards in Cornwall and a short-lived Central District based on Bradninch in Devon, brought a new professionalism to the role; arguing for improvements, upgrading the estates in their care. One employee from those years still serves the Duchy today. Claudia Payne is Jimmy James's personal assistant, but her unrivalled knowledge of the Duchy spans five Secretaries, giving a continuity to Buckingham Gate welcomed by many of the tenants.

By 1981, when Tony Gray was succeeded as Secretary by John Higgs, the Duchy's star was again in the ascendant. Farming had boomed following Britain's entry into the European Community. These were the years of plenty. Subsidies multiplied. There were grants to grub out hedges, others to replant them. As rents and property values rose sharply, so also did those in the Duchy. Development land was sold. By the beginning of the 1980s the old habit of allowing farmers to pay for their own improvements had been replaced by a programme of repairs and investment in new buildings, which allowed regular rent reviews and a higher return on the capital.

John Higgs remains one of the oustanding figures in the Duchy's history, giving it a renewed sense of purpose. A practical farmer with land in Oxfordshire and an estate in Scotland, his main interests were rural development and estate management. A varied career included working for the Food and Agriculture Organisation of the United Nations and serving on the Estates Committee of Oxford University. Despite so bureaucratic a

The Prince of Wales and Sir John Higgs (left) with John Rowe, tenant of Frenchbeer Farm, near Chagford, Dartmoor, shortly after Sir John Higgs became Secretary in 1981.

background, John Higgs was quick-witted and blessed with the common touch, characteristics that endeared him to tenants the length of the Duchy, many of whom still remember him with affection. But his greatest achievement was to awaken the interest of his royal master in the affairs of the Duchy. Despite their differences in age, the two soon established a close friendship that went deeper than the usual relationship between the Prince and those who served him. Some have described John Higgs as the Prince's teacher, the mentor who introduced him to broader more rural horizons in the wake of his leaving the Navy.

The seeds of Prince Charles's involvement in the peculiar hybrid that paid all his bills had first been sown in 1980 when the Duchy bought Highgrove House. The Duchy Home Farm was then at Stoke Climsland in Cornwall. The Prince had been offered Chevening House in Kent as an official country residence. Neither held much attraction. Chevening was administered by a Trust. The house that went with the Home Farm was small; its distance from London too great to make sense. Other possibilities ranged from Trematon Castle to Tor Royal on Dartmoor, but all were unsuitable. But the Prince was determined to have a home of his own, in which he could do as he pleased well away from the public gaze and prying lens, and one which was a part of the Duchy. Since the demolition of Kennington Palace there had never been a great house at its heart, nor had any recent Duke of Cornwall lived amongst his tenants.

In the spring of 1978, in a letter to his Private Secretary, the Prince wrote: 'It would be so much more fun if the Duchy would purchase a nice house with a small farm, having sold somewhere less useful in Cornwall, for instance, where I could learn some practical farming for a start – as well as being my own master.' Once the Prince's thoughts became known, Tony Gray began the delicate task of persuading the Duchy's watchdog, the Treasury, that the proposal did not overstep the bounds of the 1863 Management Act. Enshrined in the Act was the need for Treasury approval for all property transactions and improvement schemes costing more than £200,000 – less than a suitable estate was likely to cost. The Duchy was also required to manage its estates efficiently. Despite the long-term capital growth of any new purchase, short-term revenues were likely to be reduced

The Prince of Wales taking his turn at the milking, Yardworthy Farm, 1983.

by diverting the income from high-yielding investments into farmland, where the returns were certain to be lower.

Once the financial implications had been resolved, the search began. Gradually the focus narrowed to Gloucestershire, which as well as being halfway between London and Cornwall and close to the Duchy's Eastern District office in Bath was also the home of his sister, Princess Anne. *The Times* advertisement for Highgrove was spotted by Martin Argles, then the Eastern District Land Steward. The asking price for Highgrove and its 340 acres was some £750,000, and both house and land were owned by Maurice Macmillan, son of the former Prime Minister, Harold Macmillan. By July 1980 contracts had been exchanged. The Duchy had a purchase in need of repair, the Prince the home he yearned for.

At first, the Prince's wish to begin farming was limited to two Jersey cows borrowed from the Home Farm at Windsor to provide milk for the house. The land at Highgrove was too scattered to be viable, but once John Higgs became Secretary he persuaded the Prince that if in the long term he hoped to take up farming the sooner he began learning the better; that he ought to know the cost of a fence post or sack of seed. Before he had time to change his mind the Prince found himself sharing a remote Dartmoor farmhouse with Fred and Vera Hutchings and their son Wilf. Yardworthy Farm stands at over 1,000 feet, and in February is bleak and forbidding. For five days Prince Charles rose before dawn to help Wilf with the milking. He spread muck, loaded logs, folded sheep, turned an amateur's hand to dry-stone walling. A start had been made, and once he had returned to the comforts of Highgrove he suggested gaining further experience by entering into partnership with a Duchy tenant. For some time he had felt that as Prince of Wales he ought to own land in the Principality. When a 700 acre arable farm at Boverton in South Glamorgan came on the market, it was bought by the Duchy – a young Welsh farmer acquiring a prince for a partner. But though the farm overlooked the Bristol Channel, and was highly profitable, the Wales of the Prince's imagination was wilder and more rugged. In due course the partnership was dissolved and turned into a straightforward tenancy. In 1985 the Prince's search for a farm of his own finally came to an end with the purchase of Broadfield Farm, a 420 acre mixed farm within a few miles of Highgrove.

By then much else had been achieved. In 1982, following negotiations with the Treasury, a new Management Act was passed by Parliament. Its architects were the then Duchy solicitor, Henry Boyd-Carpenter, of Farrer & Co, who now acts for the Queen, and its Attorney General, Andrew Morritt, now knighted and a High Court judge. Until Tony Gray became Secretary the Duchy had few dealings with the Palace of Westminster, and lacked the allies in Parliament needed to win support for a new Act. Political doors were tentatively knocked on, contacts established. By a quirk of good fortune, the Third Reading came before Parliament on the June evening Prince William was born, sweeping all opposition before it in the mood of rejoicing that followed the announcement. Whilst still forbidding the Duchy to own land outside England or Wales, the new Act relaxed the rules governing its use of capital, giving it a much freer hand. In essence, the Act harked back to Edward III's original charter, defining each duke as the Duchy's life-tenant. Though the Prince of Wales is entitled to its income, which can be spent how he pleases, the Treasury on behalf of Parliament remains responsible for ensuring that the capital value of the Duchy is managed in a proper manner so as to provide for present and future dukes.

John Higgs was finally free to turn his attention to the land in his care. Those who knew him in his prime, and worked with him during this period, recall it as being as exhilarating as any in their careers. Photographs show him leaving a Somerset farmhouse happily clutching a flagon of cider, walking with the Prince through Duchy woodland in Cornwall. The two men instituted a series of seven 'Duchy Days' a year, days the Prince set aside to visit his tenants. Though the logistics of calling on as many as five farms a day, with lunch at one, tea around the kitchen table in another, accompanied by a retinue of Land Stewards and their deputies, gave such days the air of whistle-stop Royal tours, they were largely informal. There was no advance publicity, no press. Once the ice had been broken, farmers spoke freely of their hopes and concerns – some even daring a grumble about the rent. By now, the Prince's interest in

The Prince of Wales having tea with Graham Kitto at Higher Coombe Farm, near Liskeard in Cornwall, in 1994.

rural architecture and conservation was well-known. Plans for renovating a barn or building a new dairy would be scrutinized, a walk round the land prompt suggestions for tree-planting or pond clearance. Prince Charles has a keen eye for detail, noticing what to many might seem trivial: gutters, fencing, a copse in need of thinning. Time was found to speak to wives and children, pose for the obligatory photograph – most of them showing the Prince enthroned in the family's best armchair with teacup and saucer balanced precariously.

As the Prince grew more familiar with the Duchy, so also did his influence. Because he and John Higgs shared so much in common, the ideas sustaining it gradually became welded to his – what one Land Steward has described as 'going native'. In its magazine, The Duchy Review, he wrote of his wish to 'invest this ancient institution with a more "personal" atmosphere', of his belief in the sense of continuity represented by the family farm 'in a world made ever more impersonal and abstract . . .'.

Tongue End Farm, near Spalding, Lincolnshire.

But the best ideals need the oxygen of cash. In this he was helped by the large funds now available for reinvestment in the wake of the continuing sales in Kennington and the districts, particularly of poorer quality land. The Prince's Council agreed that whilst some should be invested in stocks and shares the rest ought to be spent on adding to the farmland and commercial urban property, such as shops and offices. Between 1985 and 1988 over 3,500 acres were bought, much of it in Lincolnshire, Nottinghamshire and Cambridgeshire. The new acquisitions represented deliberate Duchy policy to spread its wings and turn east, away from its traditional West Country heartland. There was then the belief that the Duchy was too lopsided, too dependent on small mixed farms, and ought to diversify to create a better balance. Though the Lincolnshire land lay amid the dykes and fens that run east to the Wash, the farms were 'wall-to-wall' corn, and

very different in character from the bulk of the estate – leading the policy to be abandoned.

Elsewhere John Higgs was equally busy. The Duchy estates requiring the lightest touch had long been the Isles of Scilly and Dartmoor. Past neglect on Scilly meant any strengthening of its links with the Duchy being regarded warily. The harshness of Dartmoor's climate and the insular nature of hill-farming have long been complicated by other pressures: tourism, public access, conservation. In collaboration with the National Park Authority, the Duchy commissioned a report setting out guidelines for the future management of its 70,000 acres on Dartmoor, following it a year later with a similar report on the Isles of Scilly. Neither offered easy answers, but they were proof of a new willingness by the Duchy to be more open in its dealings, to consult with others when shaping its policies.

By the spring of 1986 John Higgs was dying of cancer. Thanks to the Prince of Wales's influence, he had recently been granted a knighthood, which the Prince went to his sickbed to confer. But perhaps the honour Sir John might most have relished is the comment of a Somerset farmer, an old boy, now retired, who at the mention of his name rocked back on his heels, slapped the dust from his hat, and growled, 'Ah. He were a man a man could deal with. Straight as a furrow. A warm milk and whisky as I recall. We'd shake on the rent and that'd be an end to it. Good as done.'

Following Sir John Higgs's death, Martin Argles briefly served as Acting Secretary, handing over on New Year's Day 1987 to David Landale, a Scottish landowner who had recently returned to Britain from Hong Kong. Those who remember David Landale's arrival at Buckingham Gate recall him being initially taken-aback by the amount of work that confronted him. Unlike Sir John Higgs, he had not been a member of the Prince's Council before becoming Secretary and had no experience of the demands made on the post, not least by the Prince himself. Despite the handicaps, the next six years saw him steer the Duchy through a period of change as full of potential pitfalls as

any in its past. Between 1987 and his retirement in 1993 its revenues rose from £1.7 million to nearly £4 million. He was present at the birth of Duchy Originals, the Poundbury development in Dorchester, the conversion of a derelict workshop in Birmingham into the Jewellery Business Centre. But the credit must be shared with others, not least Kevin Knott, Sir John Higgs's son-in-law, who after joining the Duchy on a temporary basis from the chartered accountants Arthur Andersen had been appointed its Deputy Secretary, and who successfully negotiated the disposal of the residue of the Kennington estate to a Housing Trust.

David Landale's first task was to move the Eastern District office from Bath to a Georgian rectory in Newton St Loe, a small village owned by the Duchy just west of the city. Tom McCaw, the Land Steward appointed to run the district, still holds the post. Helped by two deputies, he today looks after a 35,000 acre estate containing 85 farms and bounded by Lincolnshire, the Malvern Hills, Exeter in the west and Dorchester in the south.

Like the rectory at its heart, Newton St Loe wears the well-ordered air of a community long used to doffing its cap to a wealthy landlord. Until its purchase by the Duchy in 1941, the

Newton St Loe.

entire village belonged to Lord Temple, whose ancestors had owned it since the seventeenth century. Despite the distant murmur of Bath, and the nocturnal glow of its lights, more recent times appear to have passed the village by, turning it into a rural backwater linked to the larger world by a maze of sunken lanes. A horse-trough and the remains of the village stocks sit on its Green. One pair of cottages was once the Poor House, another building the Estate Office where twice a year the villagers gathered to hand over their rent. There are limestone barns, a village shop, a honey-coloured medley of houses and cottages. But most improbably of all in a village where three-quarters of the population is over sixty-five, there are still two working farms.

Newton St Loe is the only village owned virtually entirely by the Duchy. With the purchase came the family mansion, Newton Park, and 4,800 acres divided between fourteen farms. On a neighbouring hill lies the village of Englishcombe, where the Duchy owns a further 1,500 acres acquired when Henry V endowed Syon Abbey. Together, the two form the Duchy's largest lowland estate, making it not only a Duchy in miniature but a microcosm of all of rural England. There are archaeological sites, a largely untouched medieval landscape, a mill dating back to Domesday, the keep and gatehouse of a thirteenth century castle, the Georgian parkland created by 'Capability' Brown round Newton Park, the village itself. But the estate is increasingly threatened. There are also workshops, a golf course, camp site, pub and sports fields, whilst Bath's western suburbs squeeze close to woods planted when Elizabeth I administered the Duchy.

As elsewhere, the preservation of so rich a landscape whilst making certain it remains home to a working community is a complex balancing act. The Duchy's ownership of Newton St Loe gives it control over who rents its property. The sons and daughters of existing tenants take precedence, but in a community where half are widows or widowers there are insufficient young couples to sustain the shop and prevent the village from fossilizing. Scattered amongst the houses are the remnants of what once were apple orchards, whose cider was traditionally given to the farm labourers as part of their wages. Some of

this land could be built on, providing housing for Bath's professional classes, who would pay handsomely. The Duchy is just beginning to enter into a debate with the villagers about their hopes for Newton St Loe's future. Some plead for no change of any kind, citing the effects of 'infilling' in neighbouring villages. Others favour additional houses, as long as they are not asked to live in them and none are built opposite their own.

Tom McCaw shrugs, posing the obvious question. 'What do we do? Preserve it in aspic or allow in new blood?'

Similar concerns were voiced by Hugh Gay, the third generation of his family to farm Newton Farm, and whose front door opens out into the village street. The ragstone farmhouse is backed by an outhouse, now the office, where one previous tenant and his wife reputedly spent their weeks, only occupying the house on Sundays. Hugh is a dairy farmer whose 370 acres long ago collided with the impact of change. Two miles separate his yard from the River Avon, the farm's furthest boundary. To reach it, his herd has to go through three underpasses – one under a dual-carriageway, a second beneath the mainline railway between London and Bristol, whilst a third is bridged by a disused railway recently converted into a cycle track. The Duchy can do little to help. But faced elsewhere on his land by a steep slope with the camp-site at its base, and his own nervousness at what might happen if a circular hay-bale should start rolling downhill, they planted 20 acres of woodland and reduced his rent accordingly.

Another of the farm's boundaries is formed by the grounds of Newton Park. When the Duchy bought the mansion from Lord Temple, it was thought it might one day be suitable for a future Duke of Cornwall. But in 1945 it was leased to Bath City Council, and is now Bath College of Higher Education and home to 2,500 students. The workaday buildings put up by the College in the 1950s and 60s belong to an era when the Duchy turned a blind eye to architecture. Nor would they please 'Capability' Brown, who, after transforming the medieval castle into a picturesque ruin, provided his patron with two lakes. By 1990 the lakes had silted up, the woods were overgrown, and the surviving remnants of the tree-lined avenues leading to the castle had fallen victim to Dutch Elm disease. In conjunction with the

College, and with a grant from the Countryside Commission, the Duchy has embarked on restoring the parkland to its former splendour. The avenues have been replanted with limes, the lakes dredged, and a start made on clearing the undergrowth.

Despite the merits of the restoration, artificial landscapes created to indulge the whims of the wealthy always seem contrived. By contrast, the Duchy's lands at Englishcombe cast a gentler, more enduring spell – something the Duchy acknowledged by commissioning an Historic Landscape Survey of the manor in 1982 as a guide to its future conservation. This is not

RIGHT *May Day celebrations, Newton St Loe, where the Duchy is beginning to debate how best to make certain the village continues to flourish.*

BELOW *Newton Park, built for Joseph Langton between 1762-5, and now Bath College of Higher Education.*

ABOVE *Medieval strip fields sloping down to Newton Brook at Englishcombe.*

RIGHT *Looking out over the Englishcombe estate. The humps and bumps in the lower left mark the site of Barrowmead, a deserted medieval hamlet. A short section of the Wansdyke follows the hedgeline linking the two woods in the background.*

picture-postcard England, but a landscape evolving over the centuries to fit the changing needs of those who occupied it. A Roman road skirts one rim. The heart of the manor is crossed by the earth ramparts of the Wansdyke, built in the Dark Ages between the departure of the Romans and the beginnings of Anglo-Saxon settlement. The foundations of a circular dovecote and medieval longhouse betray the site of a deserted village. Gnarled stretches of wild plum and blackthorn line ancient strip fields sloping to a brook.

Jim Hopwood outside Priston Mill.

Not two miles away, on a tributary of the same brook, stands Priston Mill Farm – site of the only mill on Duchy land whose wheel still turns. The 285 acre arable and dairy farm is today tenanted by Peter and Christine Hopwood, who have recently taken over the tenancy from Peter's father, Jim. A mill has stood beside the brook for at least a thousand years, and the stonework surrounding its iron overshot wheel is medieval. The balance of the buildings retain the functional elegance of the eighteenth century. The Duchy bought the farm in the 1960s, and when Jim and his wife Margaret became its first tenants they began grinding corn for local bakers and animal feed for the farm. By the time Peter had returned to Somerset with a degree in business studies, skilful marketing had turned historic interest in the mill

into its principal attraction. The first trickle of visitors grew into 20,000 a year, leading to a cafe, adventure playground, nature trails, awning-covered trailers setting off on tours of the farm. By the early 1980s they had begun a now flourishing mail-order business selling diagnostic kits allowing farmers to test for traces of antibiotics in milk. In 1990 an old stable block was converted into workshops, whose low rent and rural peace quickly filled them. A year later it was the turn of the tithe barn, then used for storage and bedding calves, but which is now more familiar with wedding receptions and exhibitions, and which last summer shook the last of the dust from its beams when filled with the thousand young revellers enjoying the University of Bath's Summer Ball.

Not every Duchy tenant has a mill and tithe barn at their disposal, and most have to be satisfied with more modest enterprises in their search for ways of 'adding value' to farming. John and Margaret Menhinick are tenants of Trenarlett Farm, a small family holding of 145 acres on the fringe of Bodmin Moor. The Menhinicks are traditional yeoman farming stock. The stone farmhouse and its barn look out over neatly-hedged fields grazed by John's flock of Devon and Cornwall Longwools, which though not prolific sheer the heaviest wool crop of any breed and are beginning to return to favour. In summer, Margaret serves breakfast to the guests who rent the flat in the farmhouse or chance on the Bed and Breakfast sign at the end of the lane. Farms like Trenarlett are too small to support a third member of the family, and though one son farms a neighbouring Duchy starter farm, his twin brother, Mark, was determined to remain at Trenarlett. In 1988, supported by the Duchy, Mark began a mobile butcher's service, preparing the meat in a converted shed next to the house. Today, his twice-weekly round includes local pubs, village shops and individual houses – for his is a round where if the owner is out doors are left unlocked, the money on the kitchen table, and the Sunday joint is put straight in the fridge.

The need for a second income has prompted the tenants of another of the Duchy's farms in Cornwall to convert some old lambing sheds into two cottages, known as Rooke Farm Cottages. The farm is close to the north Cornish coast and ringed by competitors, all equally eager to attract summer visitors. When Rob and Gill Reskelly first broached the scheme, the Duchy hesitated, nervous of committing the capital. Finally they were persuaded, and by the summer of 1993 Rob and Gill were anxiously taking bookings for roofless buildings the last lamb had only recently left. The finished cottages are more than a match for their rivals. There are slate floors and open beams; dishwashers, washing-machines, food mixers. Honeymooners are welcomed with champagne and flowers. Those who rent them at Christmas arrive to find fires burning, Christmas trees and decorations waiting. Each cottage has a private garden, satellite television, an information pack on local attractions.

That same summer the Reskellys were waiting for their cottages to be roofed, the tenant of a neighbouring farm owned by the Duchy was unpacking in a brand new farmhouse. The original farm buildings in the small village of St Kew flanked a stream, causing concern over possible pollution. The only practical remedy was to build replacements on higher ground, funding the work by converting and selling the old buildings. Slate-hung walls circle the top floor of the new farmhouse. The lower walls are a combination of local stone and coloured render. A terracotta ridge caps the slated roof. The name of the farm, St Kew Barton, derives from when bartons were the main farm in a manor. To reflect its status, a two-storey porch was added to the new house, which as well as breaking up the straight lines of the exterior give it the air of a small manor house.

St Kew Barton Farm is the first farmhouse to be built by the Duchy since the Prince of Wales came of age. Though designed by a Cornishman, Alf Trewin, it is not difficult to see in its use of local materials the Prince's own affection for attractive traditional architecture. Unlike the much larger development at Poundbury, it was built without fanfare. But it does show how the enthusiasms of successive dukes can influence the Duchy into venturing into projects it might otherwise have shied away from. If Poundbury remains the supreme example of the Prince's gift of persuasion, second place belongs to an enterprise the Prince's Council must have greeted with bewilderment when the subject was first raised – food manufacturing.

The birth of what is now known as Duchy Originals can be traced back to two different initiatives. The first was put forward by Prince Charles at a tenants dinner in 1988 when he suggested the Duchy embark on a joint-marketing exercise to sell meat grown on traditional farms, such as those on Dartmoor. The result was a short-lived and not entirely successful attempt to sell Duchy-endorsed lamb from West Country farms through a chain of supermarkets. The second was the Highgrove Stoneground Wholemeal loaf, a test run of 41,400 loaves baked with flour milled from Highgrove's first organic wheat crop, which was put on sale in 1990.

The Duchy was feeling its way in a world of which it knew nothing. Despite the premiums being paid for organic produce, the wider food-buying public regarded the organic movement with indifference. The use of the royal name coupled with the Prince's involvement ensured publicity, but no amount of coverage could guarantee persuading the price-conscious housewife to part with her money. The breakthrough came following a discussion between David Wilson, the Prince's farm manager at Highgrove, and a local miller, John Lister, about how best to earn extra money from the Home Farm's organic oats. The search for a suitable product narrowed to biscuits, but the hunt for a baker proved more difficult. Eventually agreement was reached with Walkers Shortbread Ltd, a family-owned bakery on the banks of the River Spey, who spent two years perfecting the recipes and baking sample runs of the biscuit chosen to launch Duchy Originals.

The Oaten Biscuit was launched in November 1992. The results exceeded the expectations of even the most optimistic. 'The Prince has taken the British biscuit and turned it inside out and upside down', wrote one food writer. 'The success of the first Duchy Originals demonstrates that there is a hunger for real food of recognisable integrity', commented another. Today the Oaten Biscuit shares international shelf-space with an expanding range of other products bearing the Duchy crest, including cheeses, drinks blending herbs and fruits, and two other biscuits.

Duchy Originals Ltd is owned by The Prince of Wales Charities Trust and is run as a quite separate company from the Duchy. Though the launch of a new product involves everyone, from the Secretary downwards, in an immense amount of work, the

FAR LEFT *The Prince of Wales meeting staff at Walkers Shortbread Ltd in 1992, as Duchy Originals biscuits are moulded prior to baking.*

LEFT *The Oaten Biscuit, Duchy Originals.*

RIGHT *Jimmy James, Secretary and Keeper of the Records since July 1993.*

revenue generated by sales makes no contribution to the Duchy's own finances. In due course, the surplus profits will pass to the Trust, to be dispersed as the trustees see fit. Yet despite the lack of any economic benefit, the success of Duchy Originals has done much to increase public awareness of the Duchy itself. Its products look out from shelves all over Britain, along with a label informing shoppers that the Duchy's estates 'have been part of English life for over 600 years, providing farmers and craftsmen with their livelihood'.

Though this image of the Duchy as responsible landlord and custodian of some of the most strikingly beautiful countryside in England is correct, it is also misleading. Although the agricultural land could produce the £5 million a year required by the Prince, his determination that a proportion of its revenue be reinvested in improving the estate means that the less glamorous commercial properties are the dynamo providing the larger share of his income.

Responsibility for the commercial portfolio, the residue of the Kennington estate and all development projects belongs to Tim Gray, the Estate Surveyor, who is based at Newton St Loe and is the first to hold the appointment. Over the past few years he has master-minded a steady stream of purchases, which include offices, warehouses and shops, and only shows allegiance to the West Country when the purchase makes commercial sense. Indeed, many of the buildings now owned by the Duchy have been deliberately bought outside its traditional heartland, reducing its dependency on the region's economy. In Kennington, such freedoms are impossible. In 1961 the Duchy allowed a group of office blocks to be built on its land on the south bank of the Thames. Architecturally, they were a disaster; glass and concrete monuments to the 'dreariness and heartlessness' so disliked by Prince Charles. They were paid for by a developer, and only a small portion of the rent reaches the Duchy – though in due course the ground leases will revert and the buildings themselves become Duchy property. One, Tintagel House, is leased to the Metropolitan Police. Another, the much larger Camelford House, is now empty, allowing the prospect of future redevelopment.

David Landale retired as Secretary in the summer of 1993, exchanging a small flat above the Duchy offices in Buckingham Gate for the wider horizons of the Scottish Borders. A knighthood was conferred on him in the Birthday Honours, and his place as Secretary and Keeper of the Records was taken by the present holder of the titles, Jimmy James. The name defines the man. Jovial, quick to puncture pomposity, the genial exterior masks a highly professional surveyor who has spent much of his working life with the Duke of Westminster's Grosvenor Estates. As an ex-President of the Royal Institution of Chartered Surveyors, and highly regarded by his peers, he invested the role of Secretary with a resolution of purpose that soon gave a renewed sense of clarity to the Duchy's affairs. Jimmy James's biggest advantage lay in his being a member of the Prince's Council for ten years prior to becoming Secretary. The experience provided both an insider's knowledge of the workings of the Duchy and an understanding of the larger policies shaping its future. The air of informality he has brought to Buckingham Gate has been another ally, winning over staff and tenants alike.

Though Tim Gray oversees development projects, much of the burden falls on the Secretary. The whole process is time-consuming and fraught with pitfalls, and is usually initiated by local authorities designating land that can be released for development. Because the Prince is so much in the spotlight, the Duchy treads warily, at the Prince's behest allowing a much greater degree of consultation than other landowners or developers. Though at first glance it resembles a great landed estate, the Treasury's insistence that it be run commercially means that the Prince cannot do as he pleases, and lacks the freedom of other landowners. Technically the Duchy is not bound by planning laws in the same way as others, but in practice it submits potential schemes to the relevant local authority, abiding by its decision. Schemes for mixed housing are under way in Wiltshire and Somerset, and others will follow in due course, including Stoke Climsland in Cornwall, where the move of the village school has freed its playing field for housing, and where there are already echoes of the dilemma facing the Duchy in Newton St Loe. Long-standing residents favour the proposed scheme, which by including sheltered accommodation means the elderly can remain in the village. 'Incomers' who have moved to Stoke Climsland for its rural charms are less supportive. Once detailed planning permission has been granted, the field will be sold to a developer who in turn will be locked into building to a design approved by the Duchy.

In spite of the increased emphasis on nursing such schemes to fruition, the Duchy's agricultural land remains its most visible inheritance. It is first and foremost a landed estate, a fact given added weight by a recent decision of the Prince's Council that the total acreage must not be allowed to drop below its present level. As land is sold for development, any surplus funds will be set aside for reinvestment, some in commercial property, the balance in additional farmland, adding to the estate's diversity and maintaining its roots in the countryside.

The legislation by which tenants hold their farms has recently been amended, enabling, for the first time, farms to be let for any term agreed by both landlord and tenant. Many such tenancies are likely to be short, perhaps five or eight years, but the Duchy has chosen to take a longer view. From the outset it made it clear

that it had a twenty year term in mind, giving a lead to the farming community that other large landowners are now beginning to follow. Its acceptance that tenants will have little incentive to invest in capital projects for too short a period has been widely praised – not least by the first beneficiary to win the tenancy of a Duchy farm under the new legislation.

John Down is the new master of Park Farm, a mixed holding of just over 300 acres near Curry Mallet on the edge of the Somerset Levels. The village derives part of its name from its Norman lords, the Mallets, one of the few families which can be proved to have fought alongside the Conqueror at the Battle of Hastings. The estate passed to the Duchy in the fifteenth century, and Park Farm sits close to the church, its land fanning out from the Edwardian farmhouse. John Down's enthusiasm for his new home is tempered by knowing that the move from a Devon County Council smallholding will have cost him well over half-a-million pounds by the time he has fitted out the general purpose livestock building he hopes to build. Fifty-two other farmers competed for the tenancy, which unusually for these days was widely advertised, and whose length will allow his family to put down roots in the village. Winning the tenancy ended a ten year search for a larger farm: 'the fact that the Duchy put it on the market gave everyone hope'. By freeing his smallholding, it also helped two other farmers move up the agricultural ladder.

Jimmy James is well aware of the problems facing the modern farmer, burying his hands in horror when on a private visit the

Graham and Sandra Vallis of Highdown Farm, on the Duchy's Bradninch Estate in East Devon, bear out Prince Charles's belief that the young should be given the opportunity to tenant Duchy farms. Since taking over the 350 acre farm in 1991, the Vallises have restored a derelict cottage for holiday lets, stabling the ponies of those who ride, and replanted the original orchard. As well as a dairy herd, they keep a small flock of sheep, a few South Devon cattle, and five Gloucester Old Spot sows.

Prince of Wales asked John Down how he could afford both the capital and rent and still make a living. John avoided the obvious reply, but Jimmy James's reaction does underline the dichotomy of a Duchy that has constantly to remain on its toes to provide a naturally sympathetic landlord with money to live on. In essence, the provision of an income for successive Dukes of Cornwall is the Duchy's sole function. But the present duke's commitment to the environment makes it impossible to be so clear-cut. Just as the duties of no other Secretary of so ancient an institution include attending the meetings of the Organic Milk Co-operative, so also does no other landowner in England so publicly wear his heart on his sleeve. Until recently the National Fruit Collection at Brogdale in Kent was funded by the Ministry of Agriculture. The 137 acres of orchards hold two examples of every known breed of English apple, providing a gene bank for future growers. When a change of policy threatened Brogdale's future, the Prince's conviction that the orchards were of national importance influenced the Duchy into putting up a mortgage to secure their future and convert Brogdale into a trust. Again encouraged by the Prince, the Duchy has recently launched a Farm Habitat Award Scheme, commending tenants for their efforts to conserve the wildlife and flora on their farms.

In his introduction to a recent edition of *The Duchy Review*, the Prince of Wales ended by saying that his abiding aim lay in 'trying to make sure that my stewardship of the Duchy will enable my son to take on something of which he can be proud'. Written by many of his predecessors, such sentiments would be meaningless. But the words have the ring of the truth. Since taking over the reins of the Duchy from the Queen, her heir has gradually turned it into the public expression of a private philosophy. Where it will lead or what lies ahead others must judge. What is certain is that the Duchy today is in better heart and more caring than at any time in the past, and that much of the credit belongs to its present duke.

Highgrove, with wild flowers flanking the drive.

Highgrove: the Duchy Home Farm

No-one in the tiny Gloucestershire hamlet of Doughton had any inkling of what lay ahead when in 1980 Highgrove House was put up for sale. The Duchy Home Farm was at Stoke Climsland in Cornwall. The Prince of Wales was still a bachelor. If in private he was already shaping the ideas that have since transformed Highgrove into what he has described as 'the physical expression of a personal philosophy', his public speeches remained guarded.

With the house came 340 acres. But the land was divided into three separate blocks, and there was insufficient to make it viable as a Home Farm for the Duchy. Once Highgrove had been bought, its new owner's time was at first spent supervising repairs and alterations to the house and laying-out the gardens. To keep the land in good heart it was initially farmed jointly by Prince Charles in partnership with other farmers.

The contradictions contained in this arrangement became increasingly pronounced as the Prince grew more sure of himself. Within a few yards of farm buildings filled with the fertilisers and chemicals essential to conventional farming, organically-grown vegetables were thriving in Highgrove's walled kitchen-garden. A field close to the house had been planted with wild flowers and traditional meadow grasses. In high summer, cornflowers, poppies and corn marigolds splashed the verges flanking the front drive with a medley of colour.

In his private domain, the Prince of Wales was creating a very personal world reflecting his belief that man's relationship with the natural order is out of balance, that blind obedience to what is hailed as progress is not always the answer. He would deny this to be a harking back to an Arcadian past, seeing it instead as the affirmation of a much simpler truth – that nature is a jigsaw of interrelated systems that together preserve the well-being of every plant and living creature.

The Prince's impatience to begin testing these beliefs on a larger scale finally bore fruit. In 1985 the then Secretary of the Duchy, John Higgs, negotiated the purchase of Broadfield Farm, a 420 acre farm on the far side of the nearby town of Tetbury. Additional land has since been bought, enlarging the acreage owned by the Duchy to 1,117 acres. The purchase of Broadfield opened the way forward. A decision was taken to move the Duchy Home Farm from Cornwall to Gloucestershire and end shared-farming at Highgrove. Its custodian was now a farmer.

A tour of the Home Farm is to be reminded of how much rural England is in danger of losing. Field-names like Gallows Hill, Muddy Bottom and Big Plummer call the roll on undulating wolds fringed by woodland, walls and the broad hedge-lined 'green' tracks laid out by Prince Charles. At his insistence, there is not a strand of barbed-wire anywhere. Small valleys conceal occasional patches of scrub. Every new vista seems to frame the needle-like spire of Tetbury church, itself a product of the wealth the medieval wool trade brought to the Cotswolds. This is mixed farming country, well-drained limestone, where cereals, a dairy herd, beef cattle and sheep can all co-exist if enough land is available.

When Prince Charles first took over the stewardship of the Duchy Home Farm in 1985 the intention was to farm it by conventional means. But built into his wish that it provide a

commercial return were requests that strips around the arable fields be left unsprayed, trees and hedges be planted, and consideration be given to making the farm less intensive by reducing the use of fertilisers and chemicals. He also asked that at least a proportion of the land be converted to organic farming. With hindsight, it is easy to see that the Prince had set off on a journey with no turning back. The decision could not have been easy. The Duchy's wealth might make a commitment to what was then called 'biologically sustainable farming' easier, but any mistakes would be exposed to the full glare of publicity, and the told-you-so conservatism of the broader farming community.

With the support of his new and like-minded farm manager, David Wilson, the Farm Director, Terry Summers, and under the watchful eye of Tom McCaw, the tentative first steps were taken. An 85 acre block of land at Westonbirt, not far from the famous arboretum, was set aside for the conversion to organic farming. Two years later the first field to reach full organic status was planted with beans. Rooks devoured the lot. A second sowing disappeared beneath a tangle of couch grass. The Prince held firm, sacrificing the crop to retain the land's organic status.

ABOVE *Two fields of organic oats. The broad tree-lined track that divides them provides food and shelter for birds, small mammals and a whole range of different insects and flowers.*

LEFT *Broadfield Farm, the Duchy Home Farm, and home of David Wilson and his family.*

The 'fear and trepidation' felt by at least some of the Prince's advisers appeared to be justified. David Wilson recalls both he and the Prince being labelled as cranks. But Prince Charles was determined to press ahead in creating the 'sort of farm I want', and the following year his faith was vindicated. The same field at Westonbirt was sown with wheat, which when harvested sold for well over twice the price of a non-organic crop.

The whole process of converting land farmed by conventional methods to organic status takes time. To farmers trained since Agricultural College in the use of a complex cocktail of herbicides, pesticides, fungicides and fertilisers, the switch to organic farming means setting sail on uncharted waters. Income is lost from leaving land fallow, fuelling accusations that it is an indulgence only the wealthy can afford. The long-term benefits of potentially higher prices have to be measured against reduced yields, maintaining soil fertility, and the difficulties of weed suppression.

These were the problems the Prince's staff set out to solve in the wake of their trials at Westonbirt. The price fetched for the wheat had shown that there was a real demand for organically-grown cereals, mainly for milling into bread-making flour. The yield had been small, but by way of compensation additional money had been saved by not using sprays or nitrogen. The foundation for soil fertility when farming organically is quite simple: muck. At the Duchy Home Farm this is supplied by a dairy herd of 125 Ayrshires, 70 Aberdeen Angus beef cattle, and a flock of about 450 breeding ewes. The manure gathered from the farmyard in winter is left in long heaps on the edges of fields to compost and rot, then spread in early spring on the permanent pasture. A more complex aid to keeping soil healthy is making certain that the crops grown on it are rotated, so that one doesn't exhaust all its goodness at the expense of the rest. At Home Farm, this is achieved by a seven-year cycle. Plants like clover are rich in nitrogen, which is released into the soil when ploughed in, feeding it with nutrients.

All this is understood by the parties of farmers who regularly visit the Home Farm to see it for themselves. But where the scepticism of some turns most frequently to disbelief is over weeds. Weeds are the curse of the conventional farmer, who wages war on them with every spray he can muster, sometimes forgetting that the nitrogen applied to crops equally favours weed growth. At Home Farm they are allowed to germinate, then either uprooted when the seed bed is drilled or dislodged by a harrow when the young crop is strong enough to withstand the disturbance. Those that remain are gradually smothered by the crop itself. David Wilson grins at the bewilderment of his fellow farmers: 'Most think I go round with a sprayer before they arrive.'

The process of re-learning old techniques became increasingly urgent once the Prince of Wales decided to turn the whole farm organic. Between 1985 and 1990 two further 85 acre blocks were brought into the scheme, bringing the acreage farmed organically to over a quarter of the total. The Prince had been eager to forge ahead at the outset, but had curbed his impatience to placate the greater caution of his advisers. But the organic regime was proving a success. The farm's seven staff had grown adept at mastering the different skills it required.

Elsewhere on the estate the Prince had instigated a succession of improvements to help its wildlife. Ponds like the old cart-wash close to the farm buildings at Highgrove had been dug out and cleared, and frog spawn introduced to the water. Long stretches of dry-stone walling had been rebuilt, 20 acres of woodland

planted, including a new spinney of native timbers traditionally used by furniture-makers. One wood known as Preston's Folly was thinned of conifers to provide timber for fencing posts and a new calf house, and broadleaf trees planted in their place. Another, Tidcomb Gorse, was extended with oaks and hazel, forming a renewable supply of coppicing hazel for hurdlemaking and hedge-laying.

Improvements such as these do not only benefit man, they also act as an important habitat for wildlife. A single run of thick hedging offers shelter for partridge and voles, winter food for birds, their nesting sites in spring. Wild flowers flourish in the damp shade at their base, in turn offering sanctuary to a whole range of butterflies and other insects. The hedge itself is a windbreak, stockproof fence, source of timber. Here and there an occasional tree might be left to grow to maturity, adding to the landscape's diversity and creating a second quite different habitat. At its simplest, a hedge is a typical example of what the Prince was hoping to achieve, but as yet could not effectively measure due to the dual character of the farm – with some land organic, the balance still conventionally farmed.

David Wilson still recalls the episode that triggered the Prince's decision to put caution behind him. 'We were standing in a field of conventionally-farmed barley. It had brown rust. Both of us knew it needed spraying. Suddenly he said, "Let's just do the whole thing". One spray would have led to another, then another. It just seemed pointless.'

David remains the Prince's staunchest ally. 'A lot of people within the Duchy think we're completely mad. For me and the staff it's been a series of constant pleasureable surprises'. A Wiltshire clergyman's son and now in his early forties, he lives with his wife and family at Broadfield Farm. His yard office is

LEFT *The Prince of Wales with Mervyn Dart, here rebuilding a section of dry-stone wall by Preston's Wood.*

ABOVE RIGHT *The Prince of Wales and David Wilson at Westonbirt.*

RIGHT *Black Aberdeen Angus suckler cows and calves grazing on the Home Farm. The thick hedge in the background is an important wildlife habitat. Note the mixture of walls and hedges, all with plenty of trees dotted along their length.*

typically agricultural: mountains of paperwork, a farm map on one wall, odd bits of equipment. Only the fax machine pumping out streams of paper headed with the Duchy crest suggest a royal employer.

For David, and Terry Summers, the conversion to a totally organic farm meant much additional work. Contrary to popular belief an organic farm requires careful advance planning to run successfully. Once unable to rely on chemicals, new systems have to be set up to keep stock healthy and free of disease. The conversion programme is now complete, and the Duchy of Cornwall's Home Farm is today one of Britain's largest fully organic farms. What began as a crusade Prince Charles embarked on for moral and philosophic reasons, and was willing to risk being ridiculed to succeed in, stands at the vanguard of the wider organic movement. The costs have been immense. The benefits to wildlife remain impossible to gauge – though logic dictates they must exist. But perhaps most importantly the farm is now showing a profit.

The farm buildings are divided between Broadfield Farm and Highgrove, which means that every tractor and trailer piled high with grain has to negotiate Tetbury's narrow streets on its journey between the two. Because the back drive at Highgrove is the one most frequently used by visitors to the house, the Prince wanted the yard buildings to be both functional and architecturally of interest. Opposite a traditional hay-drying rack given to him by the people of Slovenia, and liberally toasted in Slovenian spirits once put up by the farmworkers sent over to construct it, stand the winter quarters of the beef herd. Few Aberdeen Angus cattle are housed in such comfort. A pair of pitched roofs clothed in Cotswold slates cover a long low building, open on one side, built out of chalk, flint, stone and brick – all of them salvaged from materials found on the estate. Elsewhere in the park there are other surprises: a circular stone

Tom McCaw, the Duchy's Eastern District Land Steward, with David Wilson. The three researchers from the Institute of Grassland and Environmental Research (Aberystwyth) are studying the mix of wild flowers and grasses in an organic field margin.

The beef unit, with its roof of Cotswold slates and Prince Charles's own mixture of chalk, flint, stone and brick.

66

The dovecote at Highgrove, dedicated to the memory of Sir John Higgs.

Hebridean sheep grazing near the column at Highgrove. The newly-planted limes either side of the avenue were a gift to the Prince from the staff at the Duchy of Cornwall.

dovecote dedicated to Sir John Higgs, and a tall column acting as a visual full stop at the end of an avenue of limes – an avenue given to the Prince by the staff of the Duchy to celebrate his twenty-five years as Chairman of the Prince's Council.

Not far from Highgrove, and approached from the back drive, are a range of farm buildings gathered round a courtyard. Today, they house five small businesses collectively known as the Street Farm Workshops. The Cotswold stone buildings were derelict when Highgrove was bought, and although surplus to the farm the Prince was eager that they be restored and converted into workshops to help provide additional local employment. Remarkably, the five tenants who moved in when they first opened in 1984 are there still, and flourishing.

The notion that rural workshops must reflect rural skills is completely at odds with the Duchy's tenants at Street Farm, who include a restorer of carpet-making machinery and a group of graphic artists whose work is screen-printed onto glass for the tops of gaming machines. Richard Olivier was a cabinet-maker when he first rented his workshop at Street Farm, but a chance encounter with an old friend who had travelled in the Antarctic led to the formation of Snowsled, whose eight employees now make equipment for Polar expeditions and mountain rescue work. The twelve-feet-long ash sledges made at Street Farm are these days pulled by skidoos rather than dog-teams. Clients include the British Antarctic Survey, the United States National Science Foundation and expeditions from a dozen other countries, including Pakistan and Japan. Snowsled also make lightweight glass fibre sledges for smaller expeditions, as well as tents and other components. A request that they also provide specialist clothing has led to the creation of another business, whose clothes range from those able to withstand conditions in the Arctic to jackets worn by hill-walkers in Snowdonia. In 1992 they were approached by the Mountain Rescue Committee about how best to bring down injured climbers. The vacuum mattress that resulted is today carried by virtually every Mountain Rescue Team in Great Britain and Ireland.

Next door is Roy Bishop, who carves timber sculptures of wildlife, such as badgers and owls, and miniature sculptures of English trees, carving each to scale and out of its own timber. Another workshop is occupied by the porcelain restorer Amanda Chalmers, whose skills have won her a royal warrant from the Prince of Wales, and whose clients are as likely to be a private collector in the United States as the local antique trade.

The down-to-earth character of the workshops serves as a reminder that the Home Farm is constrained by the same economic forces that bind every other Duchy tenant. The success of an organic farm is measured by its ability to increase the worth of its produce, to add value. The Home Farm is helped by its owner's name, but the Prince remains wary of allowing it to be used. For two successive seasons wheat was harvested with a binder instead of a combine, stooked into sheaves, then thrashed

Harvesting organic oats on the Home Farm. Much of the cereal crop grown at Highgrove is milled locally for use in Duchy Original biscuits.

Amanda Chalmers, a china repairer, in her workshop at Street Farm.

in a barn in late autumn. The result was a supply of organic thatching straw. But the straw proved difficult to sell. Few local people seemed willing to come off the unemployment register in exchange for a summer spent stooking corn, and the scheme had to be abandoned. Elsewhere the farm has been more successful. The 650,000 litres of milk produced annually by the dairy herd is sold through an organic milk co-operative. Lamb and beef are marketed as bred and reared on chemical free pasture. The beans and a percentage of the oats provide winter feed, whilst much of the remainder of the cereal harvest is milled into organic flour at Shipton Mill or used in the Duchy Originals biscuits. A recent success that also illustrates the strengths of an organic rotation has been rye, again sold for flour. Because of its height – it grows to six feet – rye competes easily with weeds. It requires low fertility soil so fits in well at the end of the rotation, and provides a plentiful supply of straw for bedding.

By transforming Highgrove into the Duchy of Cornwall's Home Farm it in principle became the model for every other farm in the Duchy. So far, few other tenants have chosen to imitate the Prince, but there can be little doubt that his ideas have rubbed off. Every year parties of tenants from the different

Long Meadow.

regions are taken on tours of the farm. The younger ones are undoubtedly less tied to the past, more open to new ideas. By seeing the farm for themselves, seeds are sown, perceptions and attitudes gradually changed.

Part of the Home Farm's charm lies in the unexpected, the secret copses and meadows stumbled on without warning. One such place is a single fifteen acre field, Long Meadow. A tiny spring bubbles down one slope. A family of badgers have chosen to dig their set where a group of mesolithic hunters set up camp some 10,000 years ago. The remains of medieval ridge and furrow strips can still be traced. Long Meadow is permanent pasture, grazed by sheep and cattle. There are wild flowers, a skylark singing overhead, whose triumphant song seems to celebrate and define everything the Prince of Wales is trying to preserve.

Minding the Manors

Three-quarters of the income of the Duchy comes from the back end of a cow, or so it was claimed by a recent Secretary. Although increasingly an exaggeration, it is easy to see what he meant. For centuries, it was the cow that paid the rent. Even today, visits to Duchy farms have to be timed to miss milking, vets' visits, stock feeding, silage cutting, the impassable black and white obstacle that is a dairy herd in motion, all swaying udders and the swish of tails.

The reasons are largely historical. Edward III formed the nucleus of the original Duchy from the estates and manors he could most easily lay his hands on. Since then, geography has determined the best means of farming it. Once off Dartmoor, where climate has traditionally limited the choice to sheep and beef cattle, much of the West Country is rich well-drained grassland – the natural home of the dairy cow.

In recent years the monthly milk cheque has been the one certainty for many farmers, nursing them through the imposition of quotas and set-aside, a form of lunacy insisted on by Brussels by which farmers are paid not to farm. Duchy farmers are no more immune to the industry's mixed fortunes than any other, and many have tried to diversify to help pay the bills. But farming is notoriously fickle. A few years ago Duchy Land Stewards actively encouraged diversification, but now land and rental values are rising again and the pendulum is beginning to swing the other way. Yet the legacy of the search for a second income lingers on – in bed and breakfast signs, farm shops, holiday cottages. Michael Horrell and his wife Margaret chose to make cheese.

Netherton Farm lies within sight of Bodmin Moor in the tiny Cornish valley of the River Lynher. Hamlets line a maze of lanes. The school bus seems to stop and start every few hundred yards, either to drop off children or make space for a passing tractor. But the farm's remoteness is an illusion. Since 1983 it has been the home of Yarg cheese, of which fifty tons a year is made, and which can be found on supermarket shelves all over Britain. A Horrell has been farming Netherton since the turn of the century, and today its 500 acres provide grazing for the same number of cattle, about half of whose milk goes into cheese-

Sarah Barnes, Head Cheesemaker, with her team at Netherton Farm.

OPPOSITE PAGE *The medieval fields above Chetcombe Farm, Mere, with the northern rim of the Blackmore Vale in the distance.*

making. The then Cornish Land Steward was instrumental in bringing Yarg to Netherton, putting the Horrells in touch with its creator, who had christened it by reversing the spelling of his name, and who by coating it in nettle leaves inspired the publicity that brought it success. For Michael Horrell the buying of the business was a way of expanding without major expenditure. The Duchy provided the timber for a wooden building, now dwarfed by a large cheese-making room, ripening rooms, a refrigerated store. Yarg is quick-ripening and semi-hard. It shares the taste of Caerphilly but looks like Brie. Every summer local villagers walk the hedgerows gathering the ton of nettle leaves needed for wrapping the cheeses.

Farming today is as much about education as agriculture, a development encouraged by the Duchy. At Netherton, perspex windows allow the annual 10,000 visitors to watch each stage of the cheese-making process, beginning in the milking parlour.

A restaurant in a converted barn displays information on the farm and its history. The less productive land alongside the river and in an overgrown copse now forms a nature trail. There are ducks, rare breeds, even wild boar.

All this is farming in ways few would have dreamt of twenty years ago, but which is now increasingly commonplace – and not just in the Duchy. The growth of the environmental movement, the willingness of the Prince of Wales to publicly plead for conservation of the natural landsape, both have made farmers more conscious of the impact of what they do. The old adage that farmers live for today and farm for tomorrow has never been truer. By a curious contradiction, it is often the smaller farmer who best serves the cause of conservation, usually through neglect. Ponds may become overgrown, but are rarely filled in. Fields are smaller, leading to more hedges. A bustling go-ahead farmer would probably have found a way of working the steep land on a Duchy farm at Widcombe in north Somerset. But the farm's size has left a hillside uncultivated for over a century, which is now deliberately managed to preserve its wild flowers and meadow grasses.

The same is true of Chetcombe Farm, just outside Mere in Wiltshire, whose long-vanished castle was part of the original Duchy. Here the flights of terraced medieval fields that climb the chalk downs behind the farmhouse have never been sprayed or fertilised, preserving their archaeology and the increasingly rare flowers of the springy downland turf. Over 120 species have so far been counted, as well as nineteen different butterflies. The farm is run by Clive Hooper and his brother Rex, who move their cattle from one block of land to the next to reduce damage to the medieval fields. Following a visit by Prince Charles, further erosion has been stopped by clearing the scrub round which the cattle once circled. With help from the Countryside Commission, information boards and stiles have been put up to improve access whilst simultaneously steering visitors away from the most vulnerable areas.

Immediately north of Chetcombe, on the ridge of the downs, lies another of the eight Duchy farms and four smallholdings near Mere, the aptly-named Mere Down Farm. Behind the eighteenth-century farmhouse a windblown avenue of limes leads to the disused coaching road that once linked London to Exeter. Thanks to Prince Charles, who insisted it be reprieved, new oak timbers have recently been hauled aloft to strengthen the massive stone barn in the yard. The farm is tenanted by Colin Coward, whose 350 acres of cereals include an oil and protein rich variety of oats. Once again the Prince's interest in conservation has left its mark. Woods have been planted, nitrogen and stocking levels reduced, and a small acreage seeded with downland flowers and grasses.

Of all Duchy tenants, the ones to embrace the marriage between education and conservation most whole-heartedly are John and Rosemary Berry, who farm Billingsmoor Farm near Bradninch in Devon. The village's lime-lined main street hints at a grander past, for it was once a borough. Landrovers chug by in the late summer heat, trailing dust and Radio One. Outside the

pub, with its rolling Devon accents and the slap of dominoes, there is the distant hum of traffic heading south towards Exeter on the M5. The Bradninch estate has been part of the Duchy since the Middle Ages, and even today remains encircled by its farms, of which the smallest is fifty acres. Billingsmoor lies amidst a muddle of copses and small fields described in 1788 by William Simpson, the Duchy Surveyor, as 'light turnip and barley land'. Today, only the horse-drawn ploughs lining the drive recall its arable past, for the farm now includes a dairy, sheep, a handful of pigs, a cottage for holiday lets, and an annual harvest of 1,500 Christmas trees. But Billingsmoor is no ordinary farm, and any list of the string of awards won by the Berrys

LEFT *The lime avenue that once led to the London to Exeter coaching road, Mere Down Farm, Wiltshire.*

ABOVE *Billingsmoor Farm, near Bradninch, one of the Duchy farmhouses designed by Albert Richardson for George V and now the home of John and Rosemary Berry, amongst the keenest conservationists of all Duchy tenants.*

must include Rosemary's 'Farming Woman of the Year' award, presented to her by Margaret Thatcher in 1989, and the 'Country Life Farming and Conservation' awards they have already won twice. Fifteen acres of bog have been transformed into a series of ponds stocked with tench and roach, and the surrounding slopes planted with trees by the Duchy. Hedges once conventionally trimmed have been left to thicken, providing nesting sites and better shelter for stock. In collaboration with the Royal Society for the Protection of Birds, other hedges have been cut and laid so that their bird population can be monitored. Field headlands are left unsprayed, giving additional cover to small mammals. So that others can share Billingsmoor, a range of farm buildings is now a study centre visited by over 2,000 children a year as part of a GCSE geography course put together jointly by the Berrys and Devon Education Authority.

The Berrys would undoubtedly have become conservationists whoever their landlord, but nearby are two other Duchy farms where the involvement of the Prince of Wales is more evident.

The first has a recently built dairy complex whose covered yard, mixed roof heights and louvred window arches bear all the hallmarks of the Prince's interest in architecture. The second is Highdown, whose young tenants owe their future to the Prince's determination that a new generation of farmers be given the chance to take on Duchy farms.

Another farm where a fresh breeze is blowing is Higher Coombe, near Liskeard in Cornwall, where two years ago Graham and Kate Kitto took over the tenancy. At first sight it seems unremarkable. A bridge over the Looe River leads uphill to a slate-clad farmhouse. Buzzards wheel over the encircling Duchy woods. Inside the Victorian farm buildings a miscellaneous assortment of chickens roost amidst the calf pens. But beside the entrance to the yard stands a strange cylindrical dome Graham approaches with almost missionary zeal. The dome is the heart of an anaerobic digester, a sealed unit that breaks down slurry and converts it into gas, which in turns runs a boiler heating the water for the dairy and a second boiler centrally-heating the house. A lagoon stores the surplus liquid, which can then be spread directly onto the fields, saving time and damage to the soil. Once dried, the residue forms a mineral-rich compost already being suppplied to the Duchy Nursery.

An aerial view of the 150-cow dairy complex recently built by the Duchy for Malcolm and Eileen Persey at Park Farm, Bradninch, which has won the Duchy two major farm building awards.

A school party with John and Rosemary Berry at Billingsmoor Farm.

LEFT *The ponds at Billingsmoor Farm.*

Graham Kitto on top of his anaerobic digester, Higher Coombe.

Not every farmer shares the Kittos willingness to place their faith in so radical a system, indeed there are only thirty in the country. Higher Coombe lies close to the Duloe Estate, a 3,000 acre holding bought from the Church Commissioners in 1951, and whose farms reflect many of the more traditional concerns faced by Roger Halliday, the Land Steward of the Western District, whose offices are nearby. At Tredinnick Farm, for instance, such is the steepness of the valleys running down to the West Looe River that once again ponds have been formed and trees planted. A more intractable problem is a glorious range of redundant stone farm buildings. Too exposed to shelter stock, with an entrance too narrow for modern machinery, they are also too close to the farmhouse to be suitable for conversion into holiday accommodation. At Penbugle Farm, the Duchy paid for alterations to the farmhouse so that Lawrence and Brenda Light could take in guests. When it sold a barn on the edge of the farm, it met the costs of putting up a replacement. But there are problems, most notably over effluent, and despite describing himself as an 'old codger' Lawrence is debating following the Prince of Wales's example at Highgrove by planting a series of reed-beds to help purify his waste.

Such difficulties seem trifling when measured against those facing Andy and Jenny Atkinson when they moved into Westnorth Manor in 1992. The granite farmhouse had been built in the sixteenth century by a Garter King-of-Arms. After four centuries, it's age was beginning to show. The Atkinsons and their three children circled the house ahead of the builders as roof timbers riddled with death-watch beetle were removed and panelling replaced. After first being vaccinated against anthrax, a team working with lime and horsehair began the replastering.

To win the tenancy, the Atkinsons had to put forward a plan including anti-pollution measures and stocking rates. The farm is long and thin. A stream and road form one boundary. A burnt-out car dumped in a field behind the village gave warning of the problems posed by another. The stepping-stones that had brought them to Westnorth were two Devon County Council smallholdings, one of forty acres, the second ninety. But within

Looking east across the Cradley Estate towards the Malvern Hills.

an hour of walking a farm nearly three times the size they had a clear vision of how best to farm it. On April Fool's Day Westnorth Manor Farm became theirs. By September the joke had worn thin. When the Prince of Wales visited the farm he waded knee-deep through mud to inspect unfinished buildings that were already over budget. A lack of silage meant buying in concentrates. The sixty cows of their own and the sixty they had bought knew neither each-other nor the land, and the herd was only finally able to come in from the fields on Christmas Eve.

Andy Atkinson admits that those nine months took their toll. But since then their progress has been marked by articles in *Farmer's Weekly* and appearances on television. A mixed wood of hazel, alder, ash and oak has been planted alongside the stream. With advice from Chris Gregory, the Deputy Land Steward, use of fertilisers has been reduced and the barbed-wire along the boundary with the village replaced by a hedge. A stone-waller, who learnt his craft on the farm as a boy, has returned. After discovering that a previous tenant had grubbed out an orchard, Jenny replanted it, this time with purely Cornish apples, like Lord of the Isles and Cornish Gilliflower. The young trees were budded on rootstock at the Duchy Nursery, and now, after four years, the five acre orchard is beginning to fruit.

Not every Duchy farm is as beset by teething problems, nor do all depend on a dairy. The first indication that Evesbatch Farm might be different is a field filled with a lattice of tall posts not far from the village of Cradley, on the edge of the Malvern Hills. The field is more properly a 'yard', one of four in which Powell Price grows that most celebrated of all Herefordshire crops: hops. The 2,000 acre Cradley Estate is the Duchy's most recent agricultural purchase, and its rolling wooded landscape reflects a deliberate attempt by Prince Charles to buy land that is both visually attractive and farmed as diversely as possible. Hops, cows, poultry, sheep – Cradley provided them all, as well as a range of buildings that is almost a field-guide to rural architecture. One farmhouse is stone and half-timbered, another Georgian. There are bottle-top kilns, a massive timber-framed barn.

At nearly 600 acres, Evesbatch is the largest farm on the estate. Hops have been grown on Herefordshire's heavier clays since Elizabethan times, but Powell Price is the only Duchy

grower, a fact he ascribes to a pig-headed determination to keep the tradition alive. The Fuggle bines that annually climb the wirework in one of the yards grow from sixty-year-old roots. Every September a convoy of caravans from South Wales and the Black Country set up camp at the farm. The pickers bring their families and pets, giving the month-long picking an almost carnival air. In the past they slept on straw beds in a loft, picking hops by hand into hessian cribs. But today, once the bines have been cut down, they are trailered into a shed and fed through a machine whose conveyors, belts, pulleys and cogs would not discredit Heath Robinson. When the hops have been picked clean of string and leaves, they are dried over hot air in a farm building adapted for use as a kiln, packed into pockets, and sold to breweries through English Hops.

LEFT *Harvesting hops at Evesbatch Farm on the Cradley Estate.*

BELOW *Manor Farm, Ashington, bought by the Duchy in 1988, and a fine fifteenth-century example of a Ham Hill stone house. The 800 acre farm is tenanted by Colin and Marilyn Hawkins, who farmed on the edge of Dorchester until the new Poundbury development made it necessary to move.*

RIGHT *The quarry leased by Richard England on Ham Hill.*

Another Duchy tenant who shares Powell Price's belief in a regional tradition is Richard England, who leases one of the most famous of all the old quarries in the south, Ham Hill in Somerset. The hill's honey-coloured limestone has been quarried since the Romans first used it for coffins. By the Middle Ages it was being worked by two dozen quarries, described as resembling 'little parishes, so many buildings have they under the vast works'. Manor houses, churches, the humblest cottage; whole parishes along the Somerset/Dorset border were built of Ham Hill stone. The Duchy has always owned sixty acres of the hill, which is circled by the ditches and banks of an Iron Age hillfort, and is now a country park complete with information boards, picnic areas, and a Prince of Wales pub. By the 1920s the last quarry had closed, only to be re-opened in 1967 when stone was needed for a by-pass. A year later Richard England leased two acres of abandoned workings from the Duchy. Ham Hill stone is cantankerous and easily fractured: half is discarded. Despite the waste, Richard's order book gradually filled as an increasing number of clients refused to be fobbed off with concrete facing-blocks or composite artificial stone. Church restoration was followed by work for the National Trust, Bristol's Law Courts, English Heritage. Today he quarries about 1,000 tons a year, and the architectural stonework and balustrades cut and finished by his team of masons can be found as far afield as the Caribbean and California, where several months were spent working for the actor Clint Eastwood at his Carmel mansion.

In recent years, small businesses such as Richard England's have flourished throughout the Duchy, often in what once were

farm buildings. Before the Prince of Wales bought Highgrove, the old wagon shed at Street Farm was a redundant casualty of a rural revolution that by the end of the 1960s had seen a multitude of traditional buildings be abandoned. Dairy parlours, granaries, barns, stables and pigsties – all were casualties of bigger machinery sheds, farm amalgamations, new techniques for wintering stock or storing grain. By 1980 the Prince of Wales had grown weary of seeing yet another range of once much-loved buildings lying tumbledown and derelict. At meetings of the Prince's Council and in public speeches he began campaigning for their restoration as a way of encouraging rural employment and revitalizing local communities. The success of the workshop scheme remains one of his most enduring achievements. For in this the Duchy of Cornwall was a pioneer. The work it initiated in partnership with what is now the Rural Development Commission has since been widely imitated – by other landowners, county councils, even private developers.

Part of the pleasure in the ninety or so workshops owned by the Duchy is the unexpectedness of what goes on inside them. Stretching the breadth of the Duchy, from Gloucestershire in the north to the island of St Martin's in the Scillies, chance has turned them into a rich miscellany of old and new skills. A furniture maker might have a computer-based design company or maker of optics for lasers as a neighbour. One barn has been leased to the Arable Research Centre. The classrooms of the National School in Launceston have been divided into small units by Cornwall County Council as part of its Enterprise Tamar scheme. Elsewhere are a jeweller, wrought-iron worker, a demolition specialist. Robin Wood exports electronic music to broadcasters and radio stations throughout Europe from a converted barn near Truro, where he also uses synthesizers to help disabled children play music. The 32 different flavours of fudge

The North Street Workshops, Stoke-sub-Hamdon, with Ham Hill in the background.

Jane Spiers in her North Street Workshop, Stoke-sub-Hamdon, assembling museum mounts and frames after conservation of a watercolour by the Czech-born Art Nouveau artist Alphonse Mucha.

The Duchy of Cornwall Oyster Farm, Port Navas.

Len Hodges (left) packing oysters.

sold by Duchy Confectionary are made in a purpose-built stone and slate workshop near Stoke Climsland. An old farm building in the Somerset village of Stoke-sub-Hamdon has been converted into fourteen workshops, two of which are occupied by Jane Spiers, a picture restorer and framemaker, and her team of assistants. The frames are made using processes little changed for centuries, but her work is international.

Modern centrally-heated workshops such as these are a world away from an open shed perched just above the high tide line at the back of the beach at Port Navas in Cornwall. The word 'Port' should be used advisedly. There are a few houses, a pub, boats at their moorings. Woods slope down to the creek, which opens out into the broader Helford River. Most mornings a small clinker-built oyster-dredging boat laden with wire baskets noses its way into the river, with the seventy-four-year-old figure of Len Hodges beside its tiller. Len, and his son Lindsay, are proprietors of the Duchy of Cornwall Oyster Farm, leasing from the Duchy the rights to farm oysters in the Helford and the

Percuil, a smaller river that enters Falmouth Bay at St Mawes. Lindsay is the fifth generation of Hodges to earn a living from oysters, and Len himself first put to sea to help his father when a lad of fourteen.

The young oysters, or spats, take five years to fatten in the Helford's plankton-rich Gulf Stream waters. Len buys in the spats, cultivating them in beds chosen because good tidal flows guarantee ample food. Once mature, they are harvested, cleaned, graded by size, and purified under ultra violet in salt-water tanks at Port Navas. The farm's annual crop of 250,000 oysters is then packed in tubs filled with seaweed and supplied to London wholesalers and local restaurants. Len's biggest concern is a repeat outbreak of a parasitic disease that crossed the Channel from France in the 1980s and decimated stocks of native English oysters. In recent years the banning of the more lethal forms of boat anti-fouling, and the apparent departure of the disease, have helped the native oyster regain its health, and the beds are beginning to show signs of self-regeneration.

Len Hodges also sells 50,000 gallons of mussels a year, some of which are collected from the River Camel. The Camel's sinuous estuary winds deep into the north Cornish countryside, a reminder that nowhere in Cornwall is more than twenty miles from the sea – or from the Duchy's ancient rights to foreshore and river-bed. From the sheer windblown cliffs in the north, round Land's End, in and out of the coves and creeks scattered along the south, the Duchy maintains its rights to two-thirds of what is surely England's most spectacular coastline. Foreshore can vary from the broad expanse of a beach the size of Polzeath to a scrap of headland. Rights to river-bed are over those of the Tamar, Looe, Percuil, Helford and Camel rivers, extending downstream from 'the highest point to which tides shall flow' to an invisible line known as the Award Line, where it cedes its rights to the Crown.

As with farm-buildings given a new lease of life by their conversion into workshops, so also with the changing character of the Duchy's ownership of foreshore and river-bed. Ports once crammed with pilchard boats are now empty, whilst beaches traditionally deserted save for the odd farmer gathering sand or seaweed are today crowded with holiday-makers. These changes

ABOVE *Passengers boarding the ferry over the River Camel between Rock and Padstow.*

OPPOSITE PAGE *Surfers on the beach at Polzeath, with Padstow Bay and Stepper Point beyond.*

have caused the Duchy to safeguard its rights by granting licenses, which in turn are regulated by local planning authorities. Income once raised by levying a toll on cargo landed in Cornish ports has today been replaced by a range of more prosaic charges, from a concession to sell ice-cream to the trans-Atlantic telephone cables hidden beneath the beaches at Porthcurno and St Just. The Royal National Lifeboat Institution pays a nominal fee for each of their three slipways, others rather more. The ferry that plies the Camel between Padstow and Rock picks up and puts down its passengers on foreshore leased from the Duchy. Other licenses on the Camel include those granted a sailing and waterski club, a sailing school, and a group of wildfowlers.

This variety is typical of the more obviously commercial rights, but the unspoilt wildness of much of the Cornish coast, and its vulnerability, mean that the need for income has to be measured against the Prince's insistence that the Duchy do all it can to encourage conservation and wildlife. High up the Tamar is Kingsmill Creek, 200 acres of salt-marsh and tidal flats where avocets sweep the shallows for water insects and shrimps with their curved upturned bills. Such is the avocet's rarity, and the creek's attractions as a winter home for other waders, that it has been leased to the Cornish Wildlife Trust as a nature reserve. On the Helford, the Duchy is involved with a study into sea-bass by a marine conservation group, where another concern is an increase in bait-digging. Once the Duchy was directly responsible for the moorings on the Helford, but it proved an administrative burden, made worse by the occasional letter from an irate yachtsman questioning the charges reaching Prince Charles. Responsibility for the moorings has been leased, but again their numbers have to be balanced against the river's character and the needs of someone like Len Hodges, who depends on it for a living.

Built into the Duchy's rights to foreshore are its Right of Wreck, once a lucrative source of revenue from shipwrecks, flotsam, and whales and other fish washed up by the sea. The Cornish coast has not been kind to ships, nor to those who sail them, and its waters remain the most crowded graveyard in the Channel. 'From Padstow Point to Lundy Light, is a sailor's grave

by day or night', ran the rhyme, but the same is true of the rest of the coast, and there are few headlands or coves that do not mark where a ship once struck. One such victim was the Danish brigantine *Frau Metta Catharina*, outward bound from St Petersburg to Genoa with a cargo of hides, which was driven ashore on Drake's Island in Plymouth Sound on a December night in 1786. Although no lives were lost, the 100 ton brigantine broke up, finally sinking into the mud at a depth of 100 feet. There it remained for nearly two centuries, until in 1973 divers belonging to the Nautical Archaeological Section of the Plymouth Sound branch of the British Sub-Aqua Club came across a ship's bell poking from the mud. The bell was winched to the surface, revealing writing giving the ship's name, its home port of Flensburg, and the date it had been built.

There was nothing remarkable about the *Catharina*. Small trading ships of similar size were once Europe's workhorses. But because it had been preserved in a thick layer of silt it was an almost perfect example of an ordinary eighteenth century vessel, complete with cargo. The Duchy, owners of the Right of Wreck in Plymouth Sound, gave their blessing to a project to excavate the wreck, a task which continues to this day. Amongst the items so far recovered have been stoneware wine flagons, navigational instruments, bottles, shoe-buckles, and the lead seal, stamped with the imperial coat-of-arms, given by the St Petersburg customs to certify the source of the cargo. And it is the cargo that has proved historically the most durable. The bundles of hides that once filled the *Catharina's* holds were of reindeer. After being soaked to remove the salt, then dried and oiled, some were sent to museums to help research into antique leather, whilst others have been turned into bags and briefcases. The Prince of Wales allowed their sale to help finance further work on the wreck, and his own wardrobe contains a much-worn pair

Looking north over Plymouth Sound, with Drake's Island in the foreground and Plymouth Hoe beyond. The Royal Albert Bridge and Saltash are visible to the left, with the River Tamar and Dartmoor in the far distance. The 'Frau Metta Catharina' was found to the left of Drake's Island.

Divers bringing ashore some of the reindeer hides from the 'Frau Metta Catharina'.

of bespoke shoes made from one of the hides. The bell that launched the project has been returned to Flensburg aboard the Sail Training Association's *Sir Winston Churchill* by two of the team that first found it, where it is now displayed in a shipping museum.

Because of its rarity, marine archaeology is less of a concern to the Duchy than the countless historical sites on its land. It still owns ten castles and six prehistoric sites of major importance, whilst a further three hundred have been scheduled as ancient monuments. Dartmoor alone embraces remains from virtually every period in history, from Neolithic cairns to a Victorian gunpowder works. At Kit Hill, which the Prince of Wales gave to the people of Cornwall to mark the birth of Prince William, the bank and ditch of a medieval deer park can still be traced. There are mills, mine workings, quarries, field systems, canals, even deserted villages. Collectively, these range from the massive ramparts of Maiden Castle in Dorset, the largest Iron Age hillfort in Europe, to a short stretch of the Somerset Coal Canal; from the line of defensive castles built by Cornwall's Norman earls, to an abandoned Somerset hamlet known only by the fragments of medieval pottery found in a field.

One such castle is Restormel, whose circular keep looks down over Lostwithiel and the water-meadows alongside the River Fowey. After clambering amidst its ruins early in the seventeenth century, the usually matter-of-fact John Norden was sufficiently moved to write, ' ... she that was embraced, visited, and delighted with great princes, is now desolate, forsaken and forlorn.' Today Restormel is far from 'forsaken', and throughout the summer a constant procession of cars and coaches climb the track to its car-park. But Restormel is also a Duchy farm of over 400 acres, and the presence of a castle attracting 40,000 visitors a year poses problems over litter, picnickers, the movement of stock and machinery – hazards not encountered to quite such an extent by any other tenant. Dennis Hutchings' father farmed Restormel before him, and his son is already his partner. As well as a beef herd, they run a flock of 600 Poll Dorset sheep, whose lambing season stretches from October to July.

Like many of the Duchy's more important historical sites, responsibility for Restormel Castle has been handed over to

A team organized by the Dartmoor Tinworking Research Group, under the direction of Tom Greeves, archaeological adviser to the Dartmoor National Park Authority, excavating the site of a sixteenth or seventeenth century tin-blowing mill on Duchy land beside the River Walkham.

English Heritage, who annually shatter its peace by staging re-enactments of the Civil War siege that finally destroyed it, 'offering excitement, action and drama' – none of which make farming any easier. The appearance at one such battle of a cannon called 'Big Bertha', whose boom echoed out over the valley and set-off the car alarms of those who had gathered to watch, meant the Hutchings remaining permanently with their cattle to stop them panicking. A second problem they face is a South West Water Treatment Works, built on land bought from the Duchy,

Restormel Castle in 1734, from the engraving by Samuel and Nathaniel Buck.

which can only be reached by the lane leading through their farm buildings.

Such difficulties bring into focus obstacles most of us are unaware of, and which the Duchy's higher public profile means it must handle with greater delicacy than other landlords. But Restormel is a rare example of a clash of interests, and the Duchy's influence is usually beneficial. Further north in Cornwall, near Newquay, pressure from the Duchy has led to a tunnel being built under the newly-widened A30 so that Eric Comley's dairy herd can graze the sixty acres cut-off by the road from the rest of the farm. But perhaps it was Eric and Gladys Comley themselves who won over the Highways Agency? Despite tragedy and illness, quiet determination combined with a passionate love-affair with their cattle has weighed down the hall table with nearly every cup, trophy and award it is possible for a dairy farmer to win.

From the moment you catch sight of the calves, each contentedly munching outside its own straw-filled hut, it is obvious that the Summercourt Herd of Pedigree Holstein Friesians is no ordinary herd: nor are its owners ordinary farmers. For a start, the prize-winning quality of the herd owes as much to Gladys as her husband. It was she who went to Canada in 1983, triumphantly returning home with 'Moffaview Alabama', the young bull whose 759 daughters have brought the Comleys much of their recent success.

A vivacious long-haired girl looks down from a photograph on the Comley's sitting-room wall. She is smiling, happy, full of youth's bright promise. The girl is their daughter Jill, killed in a bus accident in Turkey whilst returning overland to England from India where she had been working on a farm in 1972: she was eighteen. Eric and Gladys were determined that the months spent by Jill in India should in some way be acknowledged, that out of death should come good. On a snowy winter's evening a lorry carrying twenty calves entered Heathrow, finally drawing to a halt beside an Air India cargo plane specially provided at Mrs Gandhi's request. Gift Cows to India had been born. Since then, the Comley's friendship with its people has brought young vets and farmers to study in Cornwall, inspired the creation of a special dairy unit dedicated to Jill, and taken Eric and Gladys over much of India giving advice and help to its dairy farmers.

A two hour drive from the Comleys, and the bearded figure of the Duchy's Head Forester briefly pauses to survey his surroundings. 'This is where I'm happiest, the wood I'm most proud of.' Oaks arch overhead. Dark blocks of conifer sweep uphill from a stream whose banks have been thinned to let in light. There are rides, sudden clearings, a tumbledown mine building near where Bird's-nest orchids flower in midsummer. Before Greenscombe was first planted part was small orchards and market gardens known locally for their strawberries. Now it is one of only six breeding sites of one of Britain's rarest butterflies, the Heath Fritillary. Although too modest to claim any credit, the now flourishing Greenscombe colony largely owes its survival to the labours of one man, Brian Wilson.

Brian became Head Forester in 1968, and is due to retire in the summer of 1996. As only the second holder of the post, management of the Duchy's 2,500 acres of forestry has enjoyed a continuity stretching back for nearly half a century. The Duchy's eleven commercial woods range in size from 350 acres to two. The most recent addition, Pendarves Wood near Camborne, was bought by the Duchy, then leased to the Cornish Wildlife Trust, in response to a small boy's letter to Prince Charles begging him to prevent the Forestry Commission felling 'our lovely wood'. The first Duchy plantings date back to the 1920s, much of which was felled during the Second World War. Lack of seed at the end of the war led to the woods being leased to the Forestry Commission, and it was Prince Philip who in the early 1950s encouraged the Duchy to appoint its own forester and take back their management. Former agricultural land, much of it too steep to farm, was gradually planted, usually when farms were amalgamated. A nursery was established to provide seedlings. Broadleaf trees were cleared and replaced with more profitable conifers, a policy not popular with the Prince of Wales, who is

Brian Wilson, on the edge of Greenscombe Wood: 'This is where I'm happiest, the wood I'm most proud of'. Brian Wilson has recently retired from his post, after 28 years as Duchy Head Forester.

unafraid of voicing his distaste for 'wall-to-wall Christmas trees'. Today, the woods are approximately twenty per cent broadleaf, whilst the balance is a mixture of Douglas fir, larch, hemlock, red cedar and spruce. The woods are managed on a fifty year rotation. Thinning begins in a five year cycle when the trees are about sixteen-years-old, so that the distance between each gradually expands as they need more space. The humblest thinnings are left to rot, enriching the soil, the rest become stakes and fencing posts. Later thinnings are either pulped for chipboard or end up as pallets, garden sheds and lapped panels. Mature timber is sawn and planked for general building use.

Over the years, increasing objections to regimented stands of conifer have led Brian Wilson into breaking them up with drifts of larch, often with an underplanting of hazel and holly, whose deciduous fresh-green foliage and autumn colours act as a counterpoint to the darker conifers. The shapes of entire woods have been softened, either by blending them more naturally into the landscape or by planting broadleaf trees along their rim. Beeches help filter wind. Sweet chestnut, oak, and wild cherry add variety. The Prince of Wales encourages access to Duchy woods. Stiles have been built, leaflets printed, woodland trails laid out for both walkers and riders.

Like his employer, Brian Wilson is convinced conservation and commercial forestry are compatible. If Prince Charles's wish to use horses to help extract timber from the woods has fallen foul of economic realities, Duchy timber will soon be stamped with the 'Woodmark' of the Soil Association, proving it to have been harvested from a renewable source. At Greenscombe, where the wood has been deliberately managed to favour the Heath Fritillary, little has been done that won't bring other benefits. Thinning conifers adds to their value when mature, but it also encourages insects, which in turn attract birds and mammals. A strip of pocket-sized meadows grew knee-deep in wild flowers once the grass had been cut. Their longer flowering period meant more nectar, providing food for a wider range of butterflies. The same has proved true of a woodland bank which is now regularly coppiced, letting in sunlight and the warmth needed for the Heath Fritillary's eggs to hatch. The larvae feed on veronica, foxglove, and plantain, the last of which is spreading down the rides, enlarging the habitat. Once airborne, the mature butterfly is weak and fluttery. To prevent it being hindered by a stand of young Douglas firs, Prince Charles insisted they be dug-up, linking the two main reserves with an aerial corridor. The results have been a delight. The few caterpillars he and his Head Forester once found by crawling together through the undergrowth have multiplied into thousands. In the hot summer of 1995 there were days when the rides were awash in the brown and orange markings of this rarest of butterflies.

In a recent speech the Prince of Wales spoke of mankind's need to accept responsibility for the stewardship of the natural world, of his conviction that 'Nature is not just something to be used or traded, but an essential part of the same web of life as ourselves.' Much of the Duchy may be about farms, forestry, workshops, rights to river-bed and foreshore, and the income they provide, but the triumphant renaissance of a single butterfly in a small Cornish wood is surely a part of that web – and proof of stewardship.

The Heath Fritillary

The Urban Duchy

I n the autumn of 1346 a ship called the *In Marie*, laden with stone and lime, was impounded in the Thames estuary and ordered into the 'king's service'. The *In Marie* had been bound for Vauxhall, where its cargo was destined for the sixteen-year-old Black Prince's new palace at Kennington. The Prince's authority gained its release. The *In Marie* hoisted sail and tacked up-river to a wharf on the south bank of the Thames, where the stone was unloaded and taken by wagon through what were then reed beds and pasture. Apart from the unfinished palace, Kennington was completely rural. Cattle grazed open fields divided by streams and winding lanes. The masons cutting stone for the battlements on the palace roof looked south over a lake and gardens towards distant woodland, north to the Thames and Westminster's meadows. It is a view none would now recognize. Modern tower blocks dwarf the offices and houses that occupy the site of the palace. The remaining lanes have been straightened and widened, and are now clogged with traffic. Kennington Park is all that survives of what were once open fields. The only consistent feature is the area's ownership. It was given to the Black Prince when the Duchy of Cornwall was created, and tiny pockets are still its today.

The manor of Kennington was divided by Lambeth Palace and land owned by the church. The smaller portion was called Prince's Meadow and bordered the Thames just east of Waterloo, the larger was in Kennington itself. We know little about the palace, though it was lived in by the Black Prince and a succession of later dukes. Kings Henry IV and V also spent some time there. For a while Geoffrey Chaucer, author of *The Canterbury*

A conjectural view of the Black Prince's palace in Kennington, demolished by Henry VIII in 1531.

Tales, was its clerk of the works, on a daily two shilling wage. As well as a hall, chapel, cellars and stables, there was a two storey 'Great Chamber', which included sleeping quarters for the dukes and their wives. Following the Black Prince's death his ten-year-old heir, Richard II, fell asleep in the palace after a night being entertained by Kennington's citizens, mounted and masked, to a torchlight procession, music and mumming plays, which ended in a game of dice deliberately rigged to make certain the young king was the winner.

The Great Barn, Kennington, the last surviving fragment of the buildings linked to the Black Prince's palace, and finally pulled down in 1795.

The last royal visitor to the palace was Catherine of Aragon, who stayed there before her ceremonial entry into London and her luckless marriage to the future Henry VIII. And it was Henry VIII who brought its life to a close. In 1531 he ordered a dock to be dug near 'Faulxe Hall' so that the palace could be demolished and barges loaded with its stone and roof tiles for use in Whitehall Palace. The only part to be spared was the Great Barn, which, after becoming a temporary home for refugees fleeing persecution in Germany, was finally pulled down at the end of the eighteenth century. Fragments of the palace were incorporated into a smaller Jacobean manor house, which by Victorian times had become a refuge for destitute women and shared the same fate as the barn. In the 1960s, an excavation of sections of the palace site unearthed tantalizing but shadowy glimpses of its heyday. From one site came glazed floor tiles decorated with flowers. Others revealed counters for games of dice, plasterwork painted in pink and white panels or with washes of light and dark red.

From the outset, Kennington was subject to the same feudal constraints as the rest of the Duchy. When the Black Prince needed provisions for his army before Poitiers he reserved the right to buy all food sold in its markets. Nor did he hesitate to give part of it to a priory in Canterbury as a means of persuading the pope to allow his marriage to his cousin, Joan. Elizabeth I was equally indifferent to Kennington, leasing out its 'houses, barns, stables, dovecotes, yards, orchards, gardens, meadow and pasture'. The lease marks the beginning of a more distant relationship with its royal landlords that persisted until Prince Albert took over the stewardship of the Duchy in the nineteenth century. Following the Restoration, Charles II granted Kennington to Lord Moore, who within a week had sold his lease for £1,500 to Robert Clayton, M.P. for the City of London and later knighted. It was to remain in the hands of the Claytons until 1834, when the lease finally reverted to the Duchy.

Prince's Meadow was the first area to be built over. The reed beds were reclaimed, replaced by timber yards, boat-builders, potteries and glassworks. Soap and candle-makers set up works along the waterfront. East of Waterloo, the royal barges were housed in a backwater creek where the now vanished Pudding Mill Stream entered the Thames. The few houses stood on timber piles driven deep into the marshy ground. A three-room tenement, 'wherein washing women live', stood in the corner of a meadow later used as a dump for soil brought over by barge once work began on rebuilding St Paul's Cathedral following the Great Fire.

The opening of Westminster Bridge in 1750 accelerated London's expansion. By the end of the eighteenth century the royal barge house had turned into a soap-boiling works. Nearby stood a three-hundred-feet-high tower for making shot, in which molten lead was dribbled through a sieve at the summit, solidifying as it fell into roughly spherical pellets which were then rolled until round. Although a survey mentions fields and gardens, precedence is given to 'warehouses, dyehouses, storehouses, accounting houses, breweries, coach houses, carthouses, stables, cranes, sheds and wharves'. Prince's Meadow was a meadow only in name.

One rural pocket to briefly withstand the hunger for land was the five acre London Botanic Garden, opened on Duchy land in 1779 by William Curtis. For a guinea a year, subscribers could promenade round a garden whose low-lying site 'renders it peculiarly favourable for aquatic and bog plants'. Despite

Curtis's optimism, the lack of roads and the stench from open sewers outweighed the Garden's attractions. Smoke killed his plants. After ten years he admitted defeat, but not before firing a parting shot at the Duchy, accusing it of exacting terms for the renewal of his lease 'too extravagant to be complied with'.

The larger portion of Kennington was slower to be built over than Prince's Meadow. A seventeenth century Act of Parliament enabled the Duchy to grant leases lasting three generations, encouraging development. The only house on Kennington Lane was then surrounded by meadows and a chequer of drainage ditches. Elsewhere there were a few cottages and farms, the occasional wayside tavern. Close to the Thames much of the land was vulnerable to flooding, but gradually new houses, described by one observer as 'shoe-maker's boxes', began to spring up

Cuper's Gardens, near Vauxhall Dock, in 1760. The Gardens stood down stream of Westminster Bridge in the area now occupied by the South Bank Centre.

along the two largest roads, Kennington Lane and Kennington Park Road. The opening of Waterloo Bridge led to the laying out of a new turnpike, now Kennington Road, between the bridge and Kennington Common, making the area both accessible and fashionable.

The Common was Kennington's heart. Smallholders grazed their cattle on it during the summer and fought to prevent carts using it as a short cut. But cricket was its principal attraction, with vast often rowdy crowds gathering to place bets and urge on Surrey during its annual battles with Kent. Frederick, Prince of Wales, patronized Surrey, spending up to £1,000 a match to be sure of fielding the best side and then watching from a specially erected pavilion. The behaviour of the crowd makes a modern match at the Oval seem tame. Dung was flung at players who displeased it, and one died after being hit by a stone. Its heroes were 'Lumpy' Stevens, who used to demolish an entire apple pie before every match and owed his nickname to his talent for spotting lumps on which to bowl his 'shooters', and William

LEFT *William Beldham, of Surrey and Hamble- don, known as 'Silver Billy', and one of the great figures of eighteenth century cricket, who died aged ninety-six in 1770.*

RIGHT *Playing coits on Kennington Common in 1782. The Horns Tavern is in the background.*

Beldham, 'a most venomous hitter', who played for Surrey for thirty-five years and whose two long-suffering wives bore him his thirty-nine children.

After matches the players gathered in Kennington's most enduring landmark, the Horns Tavern, which as early as the seventeenth century stood next to the manor pound and had a skittle ground and bowling green. Here lived Joseph Capper, who after dropping in for a drink didn't leave till he died, twenty-five years later. Capper was a man of habit, never deviating from a daily routine that began with a pint of wine and ended with rum and porter, and whose grumbles about his poverty were finally dispelled by his dying worth £30,000. One less fortunate patron of the Horns was a housebreaker con- demned to be hung whose journey to the nearby gallows was delayed for a final pint. Gallows Corner was Kennington's Piccadilly Circus. It was also where the crowds gathered to watch the execution and disembowelling of several Jacobites following Bonnie Prince Charlie's doomed 1745 rebellion.

In the late nineteenth century the Horns was rebuilt, provid- ing the setting for the last sitting of the Duchy manor court in 1925. In due course the gallows were taken down, and the area occupied by the Corner became St Mark's church, its churchyard and a tollhouse. The Common has fared the worst. Squatters built cottages round its rim. By the mid-nineteenth century it was described as being 'trodden and soiled by a troop of cows ... A kind of pond near one corner, and a deep ditch ... are the cemeteries of all the dead puppies and kittens in the vicinity.' In 1854, with the support of Prince Albert, it was turned into Ken- nington Park as a place of 'resort for respectable persons' – a function it fulfills to this day.

The Common's change of image meant it no longer could be used for cricket, a problem shared by the neighbouring Montpelier Club, whose ground had been lost to developers. A few years earlier the Club had approached the trustees of Wil- liam Otter, who when vicar of St Mark's had taken a ninety-nine year lease from the Duchy on a 'nursery and garden ground in extent about ten acres, called the Oval'.

The Oval began life as a meadow, in time being divided into market gardens: one tenant's lease included both the payment of rent and an annual hundred bundles of asparagus. In 1790 the roads round the Oval were laid out, leaving an elliptical nursery in the centre, complete with seed shop and potting sheds.

The Match
Lord Harris (Capt of English Team) saving a 4.

England playing Australia at the Oval in September 1880, with the famous gas holders dominating the background.

Once Otter became Bishop of Chichester and left Kennington his interest in the nursery waned. It was also unprofitable. The Duchy Surveyor drew up plans showing the Oval divided by a lime avenue flanked by six pairs of houses. Later plans turned the avenue into two villa-lined crescents, an idea rejected by Prince Albert. In 1845 the Duchy received a letter from Otter's Trustees stating their wish to let the Oval to a 'Gentleman who proposes to convert it into a Subscription Cricket Ground'. The Montpelier and Surrey Clubs had finally found a home.

The nursery was cleared and relaid with 10,000 turves from Tooting Common. In May 1845 those lolling on the grassy bank encircling the ground watched W. Fould's XI take to the field against W. Houghton's XI in the first cricket match ever played at the Oval, a match less memorable for its outcome than the dinner at the Horns Tavern that followed. The Montpelier Club failed to flourish, but the Surrey Club went on to become Surrey County Cricket Club, and the Oval has remained its home to this day. To list those who have played there, both for Surrey and in Test Matches, would be to attempt a history of cricket. But undoubtedly the most famous player to be linked with the Oval is Surrey's Sir Jack Hobbs, whose achievements are commemorated by the wrought ironwork entrance gates bearing his name.

If the Oval gave Kennington a new landmark, its arrival was matched by the disappearance of what to most nineteenth-century Londoners was Kennington's main claim to fame, the Vauxhall Gardens. The Gardens began life as Spring Gardens, and in his diary for 1667 Pepys lists the ingredients that flavour much of their two hundred year history: music, laughter, the singing of nightingales, and the presence of 'fine people' – particularly young and attractive ladies. Another writer described them as being 'where both sexes meet, and mutually serve one another as Guides to lose their Way, and the Windings and Turnings in the little Wildernesses are so intricate, that the most Experienced Mothers have often lost themselves in looking for their daughters.'

In 1728 the Duchy leased the twelve acre gardens to Jonathan Tyers, who renamed them, and began their transformation into London's most fashionable meeting-place. By the end of the

century there were walks, arbours, artificial ruins and cascades. A Turkish tent and Chinese pagodas added a touch of the Orient. Fashionable society, led first by Prince Frederick and later by the Prince Regent, dined in the painted supper boxes that lined the Great Walk, whilst an orchestra played from a raised rotunda. Thackeray's description in *Vanity Fair* evokes Vauxhall just after its prime:

... the hundred thousand extra lamps, which were always lighted; the fiddlers in cocked-hats, who played ravishing melodies under the gilded cockleshell in the midst of the Gardens; the singers, both of comic and sentimental ballads, who charmed the ears there; the country dances, formed by bouncing cockneys and cockneyesses, and executed amid jumping, thumping and laughter; the signal which announced that Madame Saqui was about to mount skyward on a slack-rope ascending to the stars; the hermit that always sat in the illuminated hermitage; the dark walks, so favourable to the interviews of young lovers; the pots of stout handed about by the people in the shabby old liveries; and the twinkling boxes, in which the happy feasters made believe to eat slices of almost invisible ham.

Gradually the Gardens turned into an amusement park, complete with fireworks, balloon ascents and re-enactments of Waterloo. 'More nightingales, less strumpets', wrote one critic. Cheap tawdriness masked a world whose heyday was over. The last fireworks and a device displaying the words 'Farewell for Ever' illuminated the south bank of the Thames on a July night in 1859. A month later the auctioneer's hammer fell on lots ranging from a 'Diorama of Vesuvius erupting' to '10,000 Variegated illuminated lamps'. Within five years the entire twelve acres had been built over, leaving only the manager's house, a street named after the Gardens founder, and a small open space recently cleared by Lambeth Council.

The terraced houses built over Vauxhall Gardens typified nineteenth-century Kennington. Prince's Meadow was the first to disappear. In 1810 the Prince Regent obtained parliamentary consent for its conversion into a new town, to be called 'Prince's Town'. The site was leased to a timber merchant who divided it

LEFT *England play the West Indies in the 1995 One Day International at the Oval.*

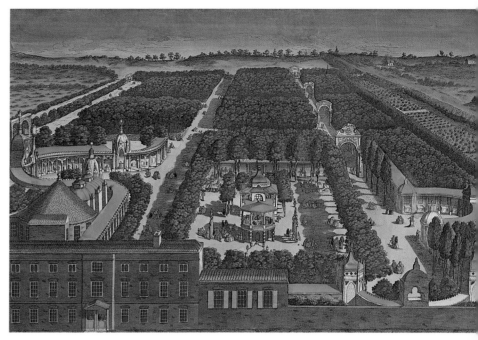

ABOVE *'A General Prospect of Vaux Hall Gardens' in about 1751.*

BELOW *A Mrs Weichel singing to a fashionable gathering at Vauxhall Gardens in 1784 that included George, Prince of Wales (he can be seen on the right in a red frock coat whispering into the ear of his then mistress, Perdita Robinson). Engraved and drawn by Thomas Rowlandson.*

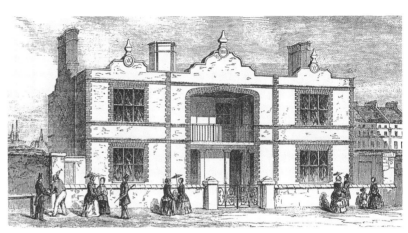

LEFT *'Over London by Rail', Gustave Dore's famous engraving of the railway arches bridging the slum tenements south of the River Thames.*

BELOW *The 'Model House for the Working Man', partly designed by Prince Albert for the Great Exhibition of 1851, and which still stand on the edge of Kennington Park.*

into small building plots. In 1823 Stamford Street had seven houses, six years later there were ninety. The estate gradually deteriorated into overcrowded tenements which the Duchy modernized and divided into flats at the end of the century, many of which were bombed during the Second World War. In 1952 the Duchy sold the Prince's Meadow estate to London County Council, and the creek that once lapped at the royal barge house now lies somewhere beneath the National Theatre.

By Victorian times the main bulk of the Duchy's lands in Kennington were launched on a slow downward spiral. The most significant nail in its coffin was the arrival of the railways, which began in 1838, and which whilst netting the Duchy considerable revenue from the sale of rights of way isolated and divided its tenants. In one case alone seven hundred houses were demolished to lay tracks into Waterloo Station. High-arched viaducts bestrode increasingly crowded streets. The elegant Georgian terraces fell in value as Kennington turned from leafy suburb into inner-city slum.

Prince Albert did what he could. The 'Model House for the Working Man' he had collaborated on designing for the Great

Exhibition was re-erected in Kennington Park. Built with hollow bricks for four families at a weekly rent of four shillings, and complete with meat safes, water closets and central refuse shafts, they stand there still – alas hemmed in by overgrown holly trees. In 1854, in what marks the Duchy's first attempt to improve housing conditions in the area, he persuaded the Prince's Council to buy a group of houses which were modernized and renamed Vauxhall Model Lodging Houses.

Many of those who set up home in the speculators' new houses were clerks, shopkeepers and skilled labourers. Commerce had arrived, causing one tenant to write to the Duchy complaining of the dust caused by his neighbour, a 'shaker of mats, rugs and carpets'. In its wake came a horse-drawn tram service, whose stables and depot were built on the site of the old manor house, and, in 1890, the opening of an underground station on Kennington Park Road. Yet despite the changes small pockets of a more elegant past endured, throwing the contrast between rich and poor into sharper relief. The future hero of El Alamein was born in the middle-class comfort of St Mark's Vicarage. Not far away, but socially a world removed from that of Viscount

Montgomery, Charlie Chaplin spent his boyhood in a pauper's garret, carrying the slop buckets down three flights of stairs, fighting hunger on a pennyworth of mixed stale cake.

By the start of the twentieth century a change in the law governing tenancy agreements had returned whole streets to the Duchy. Relations with its tenants were not good. None of the almshouses and charities on which the poor depended bore its name, yet revenue from Kennington accounted for about two-thirds of its income. It had taken much, put back nothing.

In 1886 the future Edward VII had appointed his father's German secretary, Maurice Holtzmann, as Secretary of the Duchy, and it was Holtzmann who made the Council realize that conditions in Kennington could deteriorate no further. Over the next twenty years the worst tenements were replaced by modern purpose-built flats, together with some commercial premises – such as a farrier's, stabling, storage for hansom cabs. Holtzmann's initiative was continued by his successor, Sir Walter Peacock, who in 1909 invited Stanley Adshead, Professor of Civic Design at Liverpool University, to draw up plans for Kennington's improvement. The results were radical, even visionary. Adshead and his partner, Stanley Ramsey, proposed its wholesale rebuilding, stage by stage as land became available. Comfortable flats capable of attracting back the middle-classes were to be disposed round crescents and 'ample squares – the town's communal garden'. Their main influence were the long unbroken terraces of what little remained of Georgian Kennington, but the Duchy's most pressing need was housing for the poor. The outcome was a two-storey Old Tenants Hostel built round an open courtyard. Ionic pilasters flank its entrance. Facing the pavement was a small corner shop. Adshead and Ramsey worked all over Kennington, but their finest legacies are surely Courtenay Street and Square, completed in 1919. Simple, uncluttered, with delicate wrought-iron entrances, they remain to this day one of London's most beguiling surprises.

ABOVE RIGHT *The Old Tenants Hostel, now Woodstock Court, Kennington, in the 1930s.*

RIGHT *Courtenay Square, Kennington, designed by Stanley Adshead and Stanley Ramsey and completed in 1919.*

Between the wars the rebuilding continued, though some land was sold, primarily to London County Council and Lambeth Council, both of whom urged the Duchy to sweep away its remaining slums as quickly as possible. In 1930 Holroyd Chambers was appointed Kennington's first Land Steward, a post he retained until 1964. The arrival of Chambers in the rabbit warren of rooms that served as the Duchy's estate office at Kennington Gate lead to the building of a succession of blocks of flats, designed by Louis de Soissons, let at rents equal to those charged by the council. The most ambitious – though not the most successful – was Newquay House, whose seventy-six flats opened onto balconies round a central courtyard, and which was opened by the then Prince of Wales in 1933. The Prince's concern for the unemployed encouraged the founding of the Crypt Club for out-of-work men, whose amateur boxing bouts he regularly attended.

The Duchy of Cornwall dominated 1930s Kennington. It owned 1,500 houses and flats. Despite the aspirations of Adshead and Ramsey's new designs, much of the area remained defiantly working class. Each week a steady trickle of tenants could be seen walking towards Kennington Gate to hand over the rent.

A group of unemployed playing dominoes at the Crypt Club, Kennington, in 1932.

One street had a broom and brush works, another provided seasonal work for the women in a jam and pickle factory. In September, entire streets fell silent once the special hop-pickers trains had departed for Kent. Some of the older people, Duchy born and bred, still wore blue and red beads in the belief they prevented scarlet fever. On Kennington Lane, costers cried their wares from barrows selling everything from live eels to patent medicines.

Then came the Blitz. The lovingly tended square in the centre of the Oval, where only a few years earlier Len Hutton had scored 364 runs against Australia in England's still unbeaten Test record of 903, was ripped apart by high explosives. A searchlight battery and anti-aircraft guns were sited in the outfield. Eventually the entire ground was turned into a prisoner-of-war camp, complete with huts, posts and miles of barbed wire. One raid led to the destruction of part of Newburn Street, site of both the Old Tenants Hostel and Newquay House. In 1940 George VI and Queen Elizabeth visited Kennington to inspect the damage for themselves.

The coming of peace sent Bert Lock, the Oval's groundsman, on long hikes over the Thames marshes in search of weed-free turf: 35,000 were finally laid. The biggest post-war development was on the Albert Embankment. A flour mill and the Victorian 'lodging houses' were demolished, to be replaced by three profitable but unattractive office blocks, built on a 125 year lease. Gradual improvements elsewhere led the local paper to prophecy Kennington's 'fashionable invasion'. Due to the proximity of Parliament, a scattering of M.P.s and peers moved in, one of whom installed his mistress. In 1968 a triangular site occupied in medieval times by the palace stables was turned into a mixture of flats, houses and studios set round a communal garden.

Throughout this period the Duchy continued to sell, so that when Prince Charles turned twenty-one in 1969 he inherited an estate half its pre-war size, some of whose rents were fixed at £1 a year. In the early 1970s, the Prince's Council, encouraged by the Prince, agreed that what remained needed considerable improvement if the Duchy's reputation as landlord wasn't to suffer. The prime requirement was for sheltered housing. By the early 1980s rent controls, rising maintenance costs, and an

George VI and Queen Elizabeth inspecting an air raid shelter at the Old Tenants Hostel, during their visit to Kennington in March 1940.

looked after if those who lived in it had a stake in its future, and that tenants needed to be involved in decision-making. The results have been remarkable. Over the last few years ownership of virtually the entire estate has passed to housing associations, primarily London & Quadrant Housing Trust. Today, the Duchy's residential holdings in Kennington consist of 25 houses and 36 flats, though a further 200 flats are due to be returned to it in thirty years, when the present lease to Lambeth Borough Council expires. Other properties include the Oval and Surrey Tavern, Archbishop Tenison School, the County Court and a health clinic, and a few commercial premises, amongst them a Prince of Wales pub.

The first building to benefit from the change of ownership was the Old Tenants Hostel, which was renamed Woodstock Court in memory of the Black Prince's birthplace and completely

The open courtyard in the centre of Woodstock Court.

increasingly vocal Council, had placed the Duchy on the defensive, and the pace of disposal quickened. Cultural changes and raised expectations placed the Duchy in an almost impossible situation. To some it was an outmoded symbol of the old order that needed to be swept away. Others had been Duchy tenants for generations and traditionally turned to it to provide accommodation for their sons and daughters.

Hesitation as how best to reconcile such different views was finally resolved when Rod Hackney, a pioneer of 'community architecture' and then President of the Royal Institute of British Architects, persuaded the Prince of Wales that housing was best modernized to provide sheltered accommodation in 24 flats. Courtenay Street and Square have also been sold, but in such a way that social and private sector housing are mixed in together. The grocery shop outside Woodstock Court is now London & Quadrant's office, stressing their role in the management of nearly 400 properties once belonging to the Duchy. By far the most costly project has been the £12 million refurbishment of Newquay House, which by 1986 was showing its age and was largely occupied by the elderly. To help assess what needed to be done, two architects from Hunt Thompson Associates were installed in an empty flat. Questionnaires were sent out, a Tenants Association formed, and a regular newsletter published. A final report was delivered to the Duchy, and a year later London & Quadrant bought the block, completing its modernization in 1994.

Two more recent developments have been Bryher Court and Tresco House, both on Duchy land, and both of which bear the stamp of a landlord whose affection for Classical architecture is in sharp contrast to the drab tower blocks nearby. The Old English bricks traditional to Kennington offer a backdrop to columns, porticoes and classical eaves. Bryher Court's dozen flats are designed for first time home-buyers to purchase on a part-buy, part-rent basis. The 28 sheltered homes in Tresco Court are for the frail and elderly, and include a range of tiny details to make life easier, from windows whose external glass can be cleaned from the inside to raised flower beds for wheelchair users.

The Prince's involvement has been crucial. Throughout the construction period he was a regular visitor, donning an ill-fitting hard hat, demanding progress reports, dropping in on tenants for a cup of tea or passing chat. If Kennington is no longer a royal manor, many of its citizens seem unaware that it ever had been. For me, all its changes – social, cultural, architectural – were best summed up by a lady of Jamaican descent, hair in rollers, arms folded over an ample bosom, who after likening the Prince of Wales to a more obvious hero, the Reggae singer Bob Marley, grinned and said, 'He done us fine. The kids is safe, the neighbours okay. It ain't a palace, but my man ain't a prince.'

The gradual sale of Kennington's remnants does not mean the Duchy is renouncing its urban past. Sales have been balanced by purchases elsewhere. Of these, both the most challenging and unexpected is in Birmingham, a city more used to being taken to task by the Prince of Wales for its lack of vision, and once famously damned by him for transforming its centre into 'a concrete maze where only cars feel at home'.

The first indication of the Duchy of Cornwall's presence in the city is the sign of an anchor in a street of terraced workshops and small factories. Initially it suggests some unlikely nautical connection, but the anchor is also the assay mark with which Birmingham silver is hallmarked, and the street in which it hangs lies at the heart of what is surely the city's best-kept secret, the Jewellery Quarter. No setting could be more unlikely for the Duchy's first commercial inner-city development. Yet the anchor marks the entrance to the Jewellery Business Centre, a conversion by the Duchy into offices and industrial units of what was once run-down housing and a derelict workshop block.

Externally the Business Centre is typical of the buildings lining the Victorian alleys and squares that give the Jewellery Quarter its character. What were once back-to-back houses built in warm Midland brick hide cramped workshops noisy with machines

The entrance to the Jewellery Business Centre, Birmingham, showing the stainless steel entrance gates designed by Michael Johnson.

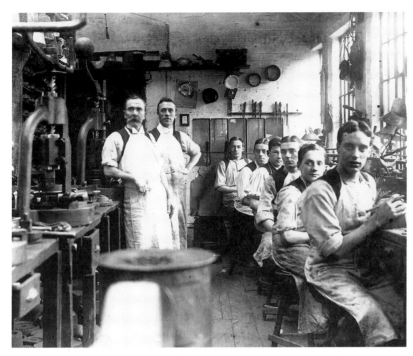

A typical workshop in the Jewellery Quarter in about 1905. The photograph shows men cutting steel stamping dies in the diesinking shop of J. W. Evans & Sons Ltd. The firm was established in 1880 and still produces a wide variety of high quality silverware.

stamping out gold chain links or silver watch backs. Upstairs windows frame solitary craftsmen hunched over their 'pegs', or benches. Birmingham's glory days as 'workshop to the world' may be over, but the brass name-plates round every doorway define an industry that has fought its way back from near extinction. There are gem setters, lappers, polishers and finishers, toolmakers, electro-platers and silversmiths, jobbing jewellers whose only task is to mount the stones sparkling in the shop windows lining the main streets. Each skill is linked to another. Smaller businesses are reliant on sub-contracting from larger ones. A ring may travel to three or four workshops before being given its final polish.

Birmingham's jewellery industry began following the discovery of gold in California and Australia in the mid-nineteenth century, which in turn lowered prices and brought finished jewellery within reach of more modest pockets. The rows of terraced houses, with their gardens and outhouses, gradually became workshops, or were demolished to make way for small factories. By the outbreak of the First World War 50,000 workers were involved in an industry whose wares were familiar throughout the Empire. When a Clydeside shipbuilder led his sweetheart to the altar, it was with a Birmingham-made wedding ring in his pocket. A homesick soldier writing from India's north-west frontier used a pen nib cut in 'Brum'. At Christmas time, workshop floorboards were cut-up for firewood, so that the gold dust and silver finings that had fallen during the year would melt, fusing in the ashes and paying for a side of beef, new boards and the first-quarter's rent.

Two World Wars and increased foreign competition led to the industry's gradual decline. By the 1960s the city fathers regarded the Jewellery Quarter as a working slum ripe for redevelopment. In 1977, at a time when planners were at last beginning to question the need for demolition, the bulldozers were halted in the wake of a successful campaign led by the Victorian Society to protect what had become Birmingham's last link with its industrial past. The Jewellery Quarter was designated a conservation area. The city council encouraged investment, renovated buildings, framed policies ensuring that the craftsmen dependent on the quarter for their livelihood weren't forced out by rising rents.

In some ways it is perhaps surprising that the Prince of Wales hadn't become involved in the Jewellery Quarter's renaissance sooner. As President of Business in the Community, he had long been an advocate of inner-city regeneration, regarding 'the old industrial buildings of the past as a real asset which, once restored and converted, can ensure the town or city has a special character of its own'. By 1989 the Prince had decided that the best way of convincing institutional investors of the potential of such projects was by directly involving the Duchy, of backing his words with cash. A 125 year lease was acquired from the city council of a derelict building dating from the 1840s which fronted three streets in the centre of the Jewellery Quarter. A grant of just under a million pounds was made available by the Department of the Environment, and the Duchy provided the additional £2.5 million needed to complete the site's conversion

into 66 workshops, a task completed in the spring of 1991. The project was managed by Grosvenor Laing Urban Enterprises Ltd, a joint venture between the Grosvenor Estate and John Laing plc, and who have since acquired a 20 per cent shareholding in the Centre.

There were problems. It was essential the external facades be preserved to retain the character of a block which mixed terraced housing, an Edwardian corner house, and the arched cast-iron windows of an 1890s factory. Local headlines incorrectly claimed the Duchy had failed to obtain planning permission for the sculpted brass and stainless-steel entrance gates. The initial hope that the units be totally dedicated to jewellery-related businesses fell foul of the recession, and though the Jewellery Business Centre is nearly full only a handful of the tenants are involved in the industry. Amongst them is Peter Lock, who despite agreeing every contract with nothing more than a handshake is kept busy repairing and hand-finishing jewellery at his tiny upstairs bench. Other tenants include a film production company, model and recruitment agencies, design companies, an illustrator, even a solicitor and accountant.

The lack of jewellers and similar craftsmen in the Centre remains a concern. The churlish might argue that as the entire Jewellery Quarter grows ever more fashionable it is in danger of becoming a victim of its own success, that those its regeneration was intended to save will gradually be driven out. Despite such anxieties, there can be little doubt that the Prince's financial commitment to the Jewellery Quarter gave a significant boost to Birmingham's revival. For the moment, the Quarter is a rare example of a still vibrant industry flourishing amidst the streets where it was founded.

ABOVE *The courtyard gardens, the Jewellery Business Centre.*

LEFT *Peter Lock finishing the mounts to rings at his bench in the Jewellery Business Centre.*

In September 1854, at about the same time as the first generation of jewellers were setting up their benches in Birmingham, Prince Albert received a letter from an obscure Dorset clergyman. Its author was Henry Moule, vicar of Fordington, a village on the outskirts of Dorchester and part of the Duchy since 1342. It was not a letter the Prince can have enjoyed. It was blunt, to the point, and completely lacking the conventional courtesies.

'God has,' began Moule, 'again visited this unhappy parish

with cholera in its most frightful form ... My conviction has strengthened as I have passed from the houses of the sick and dying, that no inconsiderable portion of the blame lies at the door of those who, for the last sixty or seventy years, have managed the estates of H.R.H. the Dukes of Cornwall.'

Faced by this onslaught, and further letters – all of which Moule made public, the Prince's Council first prevaricated, then replied by arguing the absence of any feasible means by which it could act. It was a well-rehearsed response. A previous outbreak of cholera in Fordington's overcrowded slums had claimed over a hundred lives. On this occasion, the source of the disease was infected laundry unwittingly taken in by the village washer-women from the barracks, temporarily filled with convicts. One letter demanded justice for 'past neglects', insisting the Council act to save 'their Royal Highnesses good name'. Another, prophetically, suggested Prince Albert pull down the worst slums and build new low-rental cottages on a different site. A third described conditions in which 'vice, in its worst forms, abounds', in which families slept nine to the bed, 'the drunkard, the thief, and the prostitute.'

The world described by Henry Moule completely contradicts our traditional view of the rustic English village. But Fordington was unusual. Even in the mid-nineteenth century it was ringed by communally-farmed open fields, including one of 3,000 acres. The farmhouses were in the village, along with the mill, a pound for stray stock, the church and manor court. What once had been characteristically medieval was now an antiquated survivor on the fringes of a Victorian county town. 'The farmer's boy could sit under his barley mow and pitch a stone into the office window of the town clerk; reapers at work among the sheaves nodded to acquaintances standing on the street corner', wrote Thomas Hardy, describing the rural Dorchester of his youth. Idyllic though this portrait might seem, it had a price. Because the Duchy's open fields corseted the town, expansion was impossible, and the fragment of land owned freehold in Fordington became increasingly crowded, first with the poor, then with the destitute. By the 1850s its population density was greater than that of Manchester.

Nothing was done until after Prince Albert's death. Finally, in

Fordington and the River Frome. The area in the background, near the river, was once occupied by the nineteenth century slums.

1874, the open fields were enclosed and divided into separate farms. Land was sold for building. Cheap terraced housing gradually replaced the cottages. By the turn of the century Fordington's streets were sufficiently safe for its first policeman, nicknamed the Black Devil, to patrol alone. In the 1930s Thomas Hardy's second wife, Florence, gained the support of the then Prince of Wales in a slum-clearance scheme that swept away the last of the tenements.

Henry Moule went on to become one of Dorset's most eminent Victorians. Two sons became bishops. Today, he would be a well-known environmentalist, famous for such pamphlets as *Manure for the Million*, or 'the manufacture of compost from

Looking across the western entrance and ramparts of Maiden Castle towards Poundbury, with Dorchester to its right.

human waste'. Ironically, this sternest of critics of the Duchy would now be amongst its most prominent supporters, swopping notes with the present Prince of Wales on a shared interest in architecture, drains and organic gardening. But his greatest pleasure would be the occasional outing to inspect progress on what was once an open field called Poundbury to the west of Dorchester. For the land he advised Prince Albert employ for building 'a better class of cottage in a more healthy district' is today the setting of the most controversial and ambitious project the Duchy has ever undertaken – the building of an urban extension to the town.

For a while, no Dorset gathering was immune to discussion about Poundbury. Some damned it as nostalgic, artificial, locked in an architectural past. Others, equally vociferous, thought it a brave alternative to the bland soulless housing estate so beloved of the modern developer. Voices grew shrill, the arguments wilder. Finally it was remembered that only a handful of Poundbury's 2,500 houses had even been started, let alone finished, and that it would be another twenty years before Poundbury was complete. Perhaps passing judgement was a little premature?

The seeds for Poundbury were first sown in 1987. Dorchester

was being by-passed. The town was in urgent need of low-cost housing and small industrial units. The most suitable area for expansion was on the 400 acres of Poundbury Farm, one of the Duchy farms formed following Fordington's enclosure. To avoid a repetition of the lacklustre housing built by the council when the Duchy sold it land in the 1980s, the Prince of Wales persuaded a wary Prince's Council to retain an interest in the land, instead of merely selling it to a developer. The following year he appointed Leon Krier, a specialist in urban design, to prepare an overall masterplan for the development. Two concerns dominated the Prince's thinking, that Poundbury avoid becoming yet another dreary suburban sprawl, and that its architecture incorporate the materials and building styles traditional to Dorset.

The early artists' impressions of Poundbury surround Leon Krier's creation in rolling downs and distant glimpses of the sea. We are in a rural market town, built in brick, flint and stone. Krier is a Luxembourger, with a European view of urban planning. There are tree-lined boulevards, open squares, parks, winding streets, a range of public buildings whose classical façades evoke the Roman town Dorchester once was. What no painting can show is the way Leon Krier divided Poundbury into four self-sufficient districts, or quarters, each of about 100 acres, containing houses, flats, offices, shops, workshops and leisure facilities – all within a ten minute walk.

When outline planning permission was first granted, West Dorset District Council insisted that twenty per cent of the housing be built by housing associations to provide low-rental accommodation, and that it be dispersed across each district and mixed in with private housing. Leon Krier, like his royal patron, is a firm believer in buildings taking precedence over roads. Thus the rigid geometry of most modern estates, with their straight lines and dead-end cul-de-sacs, has been abandoned in favour of a more flexible design, which as well as slowing traffic gives each terrace or group of buildings its own character. To some this is heresy, to others commonsense. It is certainly simple, and if successful, and despite having been built in only twenty-five years, will give Poundbury the feel of a traditional town that has evolved gradually over many centuries, containing buildings from every period in its past.

It would be a mistake to think Leon Krier's masterplan met only with praise. Most criticism concerned the exclusion of any hint of contemporary architecture. A few questioned the wisdom of grafting so large an extension onto a town that already existed. But most of the battles over Poundbury took place behind closed doors, as the Duchy and the Prince's advisers sought to reconcile the sheer scale of Krier's design with a scheme that was economically viable. The first phase of the development was reduced in size, the classical character of the plans exchanged for a vernacular style more suited to Dorset. Despite a slump in the housing market aggravated locally by the closure of Portland naval base, the Duchy persevered, and the first footings were finally dug in October 1993. By then an architectural code had been drawn up defining the materials to be used and what styles were permissible, right down to roof pitches and chimney stacks. Andrew Hamilton, a chartered surveyor and veteran of Quinlan Terry's classical redevelopment

The summer of 1994 and the first stage of Poundbury is beginning to take shape. The Middle Farm buildings in the background have since been leased by a company in the computer industry.

scheme on the banks of the Thames at Richmond, was appointed Development Director. Peterjohn Smyth and a team of architects based in the Bristol offices of one of the country's largest architectural practices, the Percy Thomas Partnership, was given the task of co-ordinating the local architects responsible for the actual designs.

The starry reputations of those most involved in planning Poundbury couldn't be in greater contrast than with those chosen to build it, the down-to-earth family firm of C.G.Fry & Son. From the eighteenth century onwards the Frys have supplied the small Dorset village of Litton Cheney with its coffins and farm gates, been its undertakers, carpenters and builders. Three successive generations were its parsons' clerks, daily climbing the church tower to wind the clock. By the late 1980s Philip Fry had qualified as a quantity surveyor and returned home to join his father, Eddie, in a country builder's known locally for its craftsmanship. To their amazement, they were invited to tender, and then selected, to build the first sixty-nine houses at Poundbury. Philip's delight was obvious from the start. 'Articles about what's going on at Poundbury have appeared in magazines and journals all over the world. We're working alongside some of the best architects in the country.'

Such unfeigned pleasure is made even more remarkable by the fact that the Frys are bearing all the financial risks for the private houses, buying the land from the Duchy and then selling the freeholds. Their task is made easier by the publicity surrounding Poundbury, and by the low running costs of the finished houses. Heat loss is reduced by fitting special glass. Walls, floors and ceilings are insulated to a much higher level than standard. Most houses have open fires, whilst the use of underground television cables has made aerials redundant.

The first houses completed by the Frys were those for the Guinness Trust, and by the end of 1996 all the private houses on the initial four acre site will be occupied. A range of barns has recently been leased to a high technology electronics company,

Two views of Poundbury. The top photograph shows a mixture of brick, flint, render and stone in Evershot Walk. The aerial photograph was taken in the summer of 1996.

bringing much-needed jobs. Despite the lorries ploughing to and fro along what will one day be a broad tree-shaded avenue there is already a sense of community. A postmaster, naval officer, Canadian couple and director of a local garage live within hailing distance. One enterprising seamstress in a Guinness Trust house has taken to curtain making, and hopes to move into a workshop when the builders move out. Another has signed up her neighbours for Spanish lessons. The deliberate absence of front gardens and the camaraderie fostered by being pioneers in what has been labelled the 'Prince's Poundbury Vision' has brought its residents together. Two sides of a square are being built, which when finished will provide a shop, cafe and pub, as well as a tower, which if superficially a folly will act as a focal point. Poundbury's links with the Duchy will in due course lead to the Duchy Nursery in Cornwall providing the trees for its parks, whilst some of the street names have so far been chosen by Prince Charles from those of Duchy farms.

The best place from which to watch Poundbury take shape is from a vantage that to its original builders must have seemed equally as massive an undertaking, the ramparts of Maiden Castle. The great Iron Age hillfort is on Duchy land, and is today farmed by John and Hilary Hoskin, who together with their two sons tenant the surrounding 1,100 acres. By his own admission, John Hoskin is in all but name an urban farmer who regards himself as living in a goldfish bowl: one rambler, shocked by the sight of mud on his cows, reported him to the R.S.P.C.A. Thanks in part to Sir Mortimer Wheeler's excavations of Maiden Castle, whose dramatic finds included a war cemetery dating to its storming by the Romans, and one of whose victims was found with a Roman arrow-head still embedded in his spine, the hillfort annually attracts 50,000 visitors. Though the ramparts have recently been repaired by volunteers working for the Prince's Trust, their slopes have never been ploughed or sprayed, making them a rare relic of ancient downland regularly criss-crossed by botanists in search of wild flowers. Maiden Castle overlooks the farm buildings. Dorchester and Poundbury are both creeping closer.

A reconstruction by Alan Sorrell of the Iron Age hillfort of Maiden Castle shortly before the Roman attack on the fort in AD 43 or 44.

To protect the hillfort, and encourage its flowers to self-seed, John Hoskin and English Heritage have evolved a scheme by which its 100 acres are only grazed by his sheep, who circle it in blocks during the winter. Because the farm is so visible, the plans for a new range of buildings to bed and feed cattle caused consternation at Buckingham Gate. The plans followed Prince Charles to Balmoral, who likened them to a factory. Instead of the straightforward open-span building John intended, he was persuaded to break up the design, angle the cladding to follow the roof line, and soften the silhouette by planting trees. It looks better, but cost more.

The farm is mixed, combining the sheep, cereals and a dairy with a beef herd. Hilary takes in paying guests, John chairs a local co-operative who jointly buy in their compounds and seed, and is chairman of the Dorset National Farmers Union. He claims to be a businessman first and farmer second, an image at odds with his involvement in one of the oldest of all Dorset traditions, the breeding of Candlemas cattle – the name given to cattle born within fifteen miles of Dorchester, over-wintered on the downland, and sold at a special Candlemas Fair in early February.

A second Duchy tenant to keep the tradition alive is the Hoskin's neighbour, Nick Finding, who together with his father farms one holding carved out of Fordington's open fields, and a second centred on land more recently bought by the Duchy. Nick's flair for striking deals and farm administration make him unusual. Apart from filling in when necessary, the nearest he gets to a tractor seat is the swivel chair parked in front of his computer. A two-way radio links him to two dairies, nine employees, and a farm of nearly 1,600 acres – of which more than half belongs to the Duchy. Yet the easy-going informality masks one of the Duchy's most up-to-date tenants. Wheat is sold even before planting at a fixed price. Next season's malting barley will finally flavour Spanish and German beers. The search for a crop to break the rotation and a wish to use some of the land for a non-food crop has led to flax. The pale blue and white flowers conceal a thick fibrous stem which once harvested is turned into linen or used in the paper and packing industries. In Germany, experiments with flax have moved even further ahead, leading car manufacturers like Volkswagen into discussions with

ABOVE *John Hoskin with his Candlemas cattle, against the backdrop of Maiden Castle.*

RIGHT *Clandon Farm, near Maiden Castle, one of two Duchy farms tenanted by Nick Finding.*

Nick Finding beside the board put up to give information about his farm, with a field of flax in the background.

of any field they fancied. The choice of routes would be greater, weeds find it harder to spread. Damage stopped almost immediately. Strangers rang to thank him. He put up a second notice giving information about field names, soil types, the crops he was growing. Once again the response was positive, and, in spite of the destruction of one noticeboard by vandals, his newsletters are now eagerly read by ramblers, schoolchildren, and those out walking their dogs.

Despite newspaper reports predicting duplicate Poundburys elsewhere in the Duchy, so large a development is unlikely to be repeated. A more probable approach is at Field Farm, on the edge of Shepton Mallet in Somerset, where a local farmer, David Vagg, has gone into partnership with the Duchy to build 300 houses on a 43 acre site, of which only three are owned by the Duchy. Although a tenth of Poundbury's final size, Field Farm has incorporated similar architectural codes. The materials to be used are slate, clay tiles and Doulting stone, all of them traditional to north Somerset. David Vagg's grandfather once tenanted the farm, and he was more than willing to let the Duchy manage the project and help find a purchaser. Where it differs from Poundbury is in the choice of builder, Bloor Homes, a volume house builder, who have adapted their conventional designs to incorporate the higher standards required by David Vagg and the Duchy. This is an important breakthrough. Even those most loyal to the Prince admit that if his ideas are to gain wider support they must be taken up by the larger building companies. If the Duchy's involvement in Kennington and Birmingham is a response as to how best to reinvigorate our cities, then Field Farm, like Poundbury, is an attempt at solving an equally intractable problem – how to build in the countryside without also destroying it.

the government about planting it for the production of car panels.

Like John Hoskin, much of Nick Finding's land borders Dorchester. A few years ago, in an attempt to reduce damage to crops done by walkers crossing fields without footpaths, Nick put up a noticeboard inviting people to walk round the perimeter

The Isles of Scilly

A few minutes after passing over Land's End the clouds fell away. Sunlight glinted off the sea, a lone trawler heading home with its catch. The helicopter altered course. Suddenly there was surf over rocks, a thin ribbon of sand. The sea shallowed to a Caribbean blue. More rocks, then a muddle of islands, some bare, some patched with green. A larger island came into view. Almost without warning the helicopter slowed to a halt, rotor blades clattering as it lowered itself down to the grass below. . . .

A mile or so away, on another of the islands that make up the Isles of Scilly, the two fishermen cutting new timbers for a fishing boat paid no attention to the helicopter as it swept in over Tresco to land its cargo of passengers near the famous sub-tropical gardens. This was Bryher, and John Pender and Len Jenkins were getting ready to relaunch John's crabbing-boat, the *Star of Scillonia*, which after a winter pulled up on the beach and thirty-three seasons at sea was beginning to show its age.

Finally John glanced up from the scuppers, a burly bearded figure sprouting tufts of hair from under his cap: 'Duchy? We're all Duchy here. No ifs or buts about it.'

Len grunted agreement. There was a time when nearly everyone on Bryher was a Jenkins. New blood and the arrival of 'incomers' may have added to its stock of names, but at nearly eighty Len is the oldest of the island's seventy inhabitants and can remember when Bryher, like all of the Isles of Scilly, was leased by the Duchy of Cornwall to a single family.

'Duchy did nothing for us then. We built our own houses, road, reading room. Did it all.'

'And if you don't stop soon, it'll stop you', added John with a grin.

Even in the spring sunshine Bryher was nearly deserted. Granite cottages nestled alongside a lane. A few sheds, a tractor or two, a handful of miniature high-hedged fields sloped uphill into bracken and scrub. Out to sea, gulls skimmed the narrow channel separating Bryher from its neighbour. As a boy Len rose in darkness to milk five cows, breakfasting at dawn before helping his father pull pots off Bishop Rock, six miles away in the open Atlantic. By ten he was ashore again, having collected the mail from Tresco. The rest of the day was spent on the family's eleven-acre holding, lifting flower bulbs, cutting hay, digging potatoes.

All that has changed. Len has handed over his duties as Bryher's boatman to his son. The bulk of John's catch of crabs and lobsters ends up in Spain. Today, fishing and farming provide only a fraction of Scilly's income, the bulk comes from tourism. Throughout the summer holiday-makers fill the guest-houses on St Mary's, the largest of the islands, and the cottages on its five smaller neighbours, the 'off-islands'. Visiting yachts drop anchor in their lee. Launches ply to and fro, piled high with shrimping nets, squealing children, the endless procession of visitors willing to risk the two-and-a-half hour ferry passage from Penzance. Virtually all of Scilly belongs to the Duchy of Cornwall, and the islands one Elizabethan visitor described as 'few men be glad to inhabit' are today regarded as a jewel in its crown.

Few jewels sparkle so brightly as this remote cluster of islands

The Isles of Scilly from the air, with St Mary's in the foreground, and Bryher, Tresco and St Martin's running from left to right in the distance.

nearly thirty miles south-west of Land's End. The winters are mild and usually frost-free, the surrounding seas almost translucent. There are puffins, seals, a patchwork of fields that from October to March yield the daffodils and narcissi that remain Scilly's best-known export. Visitors take away memories of white sandy beaches, rocky headlands, an impressionist palette of gorse and thrift tumbling to the sea. Scillonians know better. Salt-laden gales can batter the islands. Places like Hell Bay, Sharp Rock and Tearing Ledge are aptly named. Every graveyard is a record of ships wrecked and lives lost.

The archipelago consists of about 150 islands, of which six are inhabited. Most of the population of just over 2,000 live on St Mary's, which at five miles by three is Scilly's commercial and administrative capital. Tresco is the second largest island, and since 1834 has been leased to the Dorrien Smith family, who over successive generations have planted the trees and created the gardens that give Tresco its character. On one side lies Bryher, on the other St Martin's. To the west of St Mary's are the two most remote outposts of the entire British Isles, St Agnes and Gugh, which at low tide are linked by a sand spit. Gugh has two houses, St Agnes a population of 50.

Scilly's isolation has made it close-knit and independent. Much of its history has been one of hardship and poverty. Only in the last hundred years have flower-growing and tourism brought a modest prosperity. Even today fog and storm can cut the islands off from the mainland for days at a time. Until 1920 the Duchy's stewardship of Scilly was conducted by lessees, and Duchy officials seldom visited the islands. The result was resentment and a sense of grievance whose echoes can still be heard. Every new Land Steward is measured against his predecessor, lest the new broom he be bringing sweep where unwelcome. Any hint of

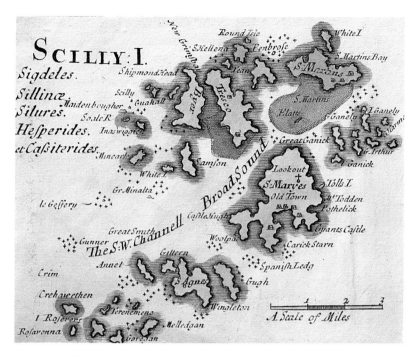

The Isles of Scilly. The map above is by Robert Morden and is taken from the 'Smaller Islands in the British Ocean', 1695.

The view west from near the quay at Lower Town, St Martin's, towards the small sandy bay at Tean with Tresco in the distance.

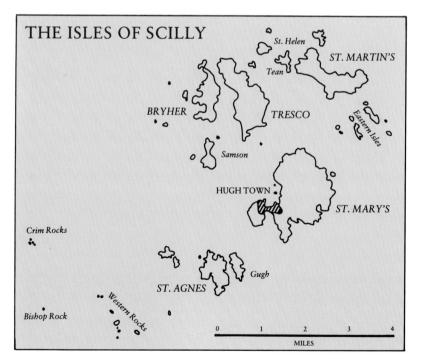

interference or change is regarded with wariness. In no two conversations concerning the Duchy are opinions the same. One might grumble about 'outsiders' telling him what to do. His neighbour applaud the Duchy as Scilly's greatest ally, the only organization capable of preserving its beauty and preventing the islands growing too commercial.

Scilly has been part of the Duchy since its fourteenth century foundation. There was then a priory on Tresco which belonged to Tavistock Abbey. Smaller islands, now uninhabited, boasted tiny chapels or hermitages, near where in prehistoric times Bronze and Iron Age settlers buried their dead in stone-covered chambers. The Romans followed, as did the Vikings. By the Middle Ages St Mary's and St Agnes were in the hands of the Blanchminster family, for which they paid the Duchy an annual rent of 400 puffins. Piracy and lawlessness prevailed. The few islanders eked out a precarious hand-to-mouth existence. Following the Dissolution of the Monasteries Tresco reverted to the

113

Hugh Town and the Garrison, St Mary's. Star Castle has been a hotel since 1933, when its first lunch guest was Edward, Prince of Wales (later Edward VIII). Hugh House, the Duchy's headquarters on Scilly, sits behind a half-moon lawn overlooking the Garrison wall on the left.

St Mary's Pool, showing the quay and Star Castle in about 1670.

Duchy, and St Mary's was leased to Thomas Seymour, later Lord Admiral, who after Henry VIII's death married his widow, Catherine Parr. Seymour was buccaneering and unscrupulous. He also sought to marry Princess Elizabeth, and was therefore a threat to the crown. Afraid that he might use the 'strong and dangerous Scilly Isles' as a refuge, he was found guilty of treason in 1549 and led out onto the scaffold.

A few years later, in 1571, Elizabeth I granted Scilly to Francis Godolphin for thirty-seven years at an annual £20 rent, forging a link between the islands and one of Cornwall's most influential families that lasted until 1831. The arrival of the Godolphins marked a change in Scillonian fortunes. Land was divided into plots, settlers encouraged. On instructions from the queen, the new Governor built a castle in the shape of an eight-pointed star on the high ground overlooking the entrance to St Mary's harbour. The surrounding promontory became a fortress known as the Garrison, with defensive walls and cannon emplacements.

Star Castle still stands, and is today a hotel leased from the Duchy by John and Mary Nicholls. John is also the Secretary of the lifeboat station and the Duchy pilot, responsible for guiding in the two dozen or so cruise ships that annually visit the islands. They can range from the 37,000 ton *Europa* down to much smaller vessels for whom Scilly, and Tresco's gardens, are an overnight anchorage on voyages that may begin in the Mediterranean and end on Scotland's west coast. Other piloting duties include bringing in tugs towing barges laden with stone for repairing sea defences or nursing foreign trawlers to safety.

The quay trawlermen tie-up alongside today is a descendant of one built by Francis Godolphin in 1601. He sited it in St Mary's Pool, close to a narrow neck of land dividing the Garrison from the rest of St Mary's. Its construction, and the protection of the castle's guns, led the islanders to abandon their original settlement and build Hugh Town, St Mary's capital and still its only town. The Civil War brought the future Charles II into brief and uncomfortable exile in Star Castle, after which the islands were occupied by Parliament.

In the wake of their victory, as elsewhere in the Duchy, Parliamentary Commissioners landed on Scilly to establish its value.

Their findings were bleak. St Martin's had two inhabitants. St Mary's was 'impoverished by troubles', its 'boats and tackles decayed by pirates and war'. Feudal rights long abandoned on other Duchy estates still survived. No one could leave the islands without the Governor's permission. Fishermen were compelled to land their catch on St Mary's, where they were paid an agreed price at the end of each season in return for the Godolphins retaining a tenth of its value.

Nor did the future bring any improvement. Despite Francis Godolphin's grandson being appointed Governor and Lord Proprietor following the Restoration in 1660, the next 150 years marked a low ebb in Scillonian fortunes. Both the Duchy and Godolphins thought Scilly worthless. One Godolphin became Dean of St Paul's, another an earl and Queen Anne's Prime Minister. The death of the last of the Godolphins led to the lease passing to a son-in-law, the 5th Duke of Leeds, who in turn left it to his heir. The Isles of Scilly had become just another pawn to be passed from one absentee landlord to the next.

Neglect did little to improve the islanders' lot. They were ruled by a steward and Council of Twelve, one of which was disbanded for 'encouraging Vice instead of preventing it'. The sea provided one harvest, the thin acid soil another. When either failed, the main diet was limpets, or 'sea beef', which though rubbery were boiled and eaten by the thousand. There were a few cattle, some pigs and sheep. Many houses were overcrowded hovels, and by the end of the eighteenth century the population was higher than today. Leases were held by unwritten agreement. On a tenant's death, the land was divided between any of the family who wanted a share, so that each holding consisted of scattered unworkable strips. Apart from dried fish, the only export was kelp, which in summer was burnt in pits, leaving an ash rich in iodine to be shipped to the mainland for use in glass and soap-making. A more fortuitous source of profit was wrecks. One probably apocryphal tale has St Mary's parson being interrupted in mid-sermon with news of a French merchantman swept ashore after a westerly gale. As his congregation hurried from their pews, the hapless cleric is reputed to have shed his surplice, jumped from the pulpit and implored the others to wait, crying, 'Let us all start fair!'

Threatened with starvation, the islanders turned to smuggling and mainland charity. 'Do not leave us to perish for lack of bread', pleaded one petition, leading to a hand-out of food and clothing and a short-lived attempt to set-up a pilchard curing industry on Tresco. As Scilly's plight worsened into a national scandal, the Duke of Leeds informed the Duchy of his unwillingness to renew his lease. In 1831 the Godolphins 260 year rule finally came to an end. For the next three years the islands tottered from one crisis to the next. The Duchy sent its surveyor, Edward Driver, to prepare a report into the state of the islands. He found rents to be hopelessly in arrears. The commander of the garrison was pocketing the harbour dues. Houses had been built without agreement. Driver's brother, George, was installed in St Mary's in an attempt to reassert the Duchy's authority, but the sharp rent increases he tried to force through only made matters worse, creating an animosity that long outlived him.

In the midst of this confusion, an unheralded passenger stepped ashore on St Mary's from the weekly sailing packet. Guided by a young boy, the mysterious stranger explored St Mary's and the off-islands, finally departing with as little ceremony as he had landed. His name was Augustus Smith, a Hertfordshire landowner who had first begun negotiations with the Duchy about taking over the Duke of Leeds lease a few years earlier. The Smiths owed their wealth to banking, but though Augustus was not yet thirty and rich enough never to work he had no appetite for fashionable leisure. Attempts to encourage reforms on the family estate had persuaded him that if handled firmly a group of paupers could become self-supporting. Delays in the negotiations led him to look elsewhere to test his theories. For a while he considered leasing the Aran Isles off Ireland's west coast, then the Duchy renewed contact. In November 1834, on a one-off payment of £20,000, an annual rent of £40, and the promise to spend £5,000 on a new pier and St Mary's still incomplete church, Augustus Smith took possession of the Isles of Scilly on a ninety-nine year lease, or three lives.

Augustus returned to Scilly early in the following year, setting up temporary home in Hugh House, once the officers' quarters in the Garrison and today the offices of the Duchy of Cornwall. His first act as Lord Proprietor was to return ten per cent of the most

Augustus Smith in about 1870.

Tresco Abbey from Abbey Pool.

recently paid rent, a gesture that lulled the islanders into thinking their new landlord likely to be sympathetic. They were soon disillusioned. Augustus's reign – in all but name he was Scilly's monarch – was to prove the most autocratic the islands had ever experienced. As with opinions about the Duchy, so also with Augustus. To some he remains a hard-hearted despot who rode rough-shod over any who stood in his way, others regard him as a far-sighted visionary who sowed the seeds of Scilly's prosperity. What is certain is that within months of his arrival the very sight of him, in tall grey hat, reefer jacket, a telescope slung over one shoulder, was sufficient to strike terror into the stoutest heart.

Augustus's first move was to build a house for himself on Tresco, the Abbey, not far from the priory ruins. To clear the site, three cottages were demolished. Discontent turned to defiance. Workmen went on strike for higher wages; vandals threw stones at the Abbey's first windows. By the time the Abbey

was completed in 1838 Augustus's determination to make Scilly self-sufficient had fostered a succession of drastic reforms, none of them popular. The old practice of dividing up land was abolished, each tenant's boundaries redrawn to make his holding more compact. Henceforth, only one member of a family could succeed to a tenancy; the rest had to make their own way in the world – either by going to sea, entering service, or learning a trade. No marriages were allowed unless a house was available. Sub-letting was forbidden, as was taking in lodgers. Paupers were deported to the mainland, where in time they were joined by any who dared question Augustus's authority. He was at his most implacable on Samson, a tiny island between St Mary's and Bryher, whose five families were forced to leave and their cottages pulled down.

As the shelter belts of trees planted by Augustus on Tresco began to rise round the terraced gardens he had started planting near the Abbey, so also did his policies begin to bear fruit. The construction of the new pier and church on St Mary's provided jobs. Roads and walls were built. Ship-building yards lined the foreshore at Hugh Town. Waste ground was cleared of stones and planted with early potatoes. Thirty years before education became obligatory on the mainland, he made it compulsory on Scilly, charging each child a penny a week to attend the schools he built and twopence if any played truant.

Within seventeen years of first setting foot on the islands, Augustus's rule had transformed them. ' ... the land was cultivated like a garden and the port was full of ships; churches were crowded with devout and well-dressed congregations. Smuggling and wrecking were unknown', wrote one admiring visitor. As Augustus grew older, relations between the islanders and their increasingly paternal landlord slowly improved. Once a year, after paying the rent, the tenants were treated to a slap-up dinner in Star Castle. Sons sat in the same seats as their fathers before them, and Augustus always joined in the carving. The loyal toast was followed by one to the 'Governor' – as the islanders called him – and a parting drink 'to our next merry meeting'.

Despite the toasts to his royal landlord, Augustus's relations with the Duchy grew increasingly acrimonious. In 1847, accompanied by Prince Albert and the young Prince of Wales, the Queen stepped ashore on St Mary's on her way north to Scotland by sea. The two princes went bird-spotting on Samson, where a gull gave the future Edward VII 'a harder nip than anything he might expect from his theatrical lady-friends in later life'. The Royal Visit prematurely ended when Augustus's coachman took the pony-carriage bearing his queen down a hill so steep she disembarked in panic, hurrying back to the safety of the Royal Yacht. Prince Albert's determination to increase the Duchy's income from the islands clashed with Augustus's belief that the Duchy had shown little gratitude for all he had done, and spent, on bringing prosperity to Scilly. The Prince thought the annual rent of £40 too low, and tried to claim the rights to anything not specifically mentioned in the lease. Augustus's letters are increasingly peppered with references to the 'shabby tricky ways' of the 'damned Duchy', and the 'greedy and title-seeking officials' who were making his life such a misery.

Augustus never married, and though gossip warmed his bed with a succession of island women, at least two of whom may have borne him children, he had no son to inherit his tenancy. The Management Act of 1863 abolished the renewal of leases based on lives, giving rise to fears that on his death the islands would revert to the Duchy, who would then benefit from the fortune he had spent on them. More than once he debated cutting his losses and leaving, but eventually he negotiated a new thirty-one year lease.

A few years later Augustus mentioned to a St Mary's farmer called William Trevellick that a box of wild daffodils he had sent to Covent Garden as an experiment had sold for a pound. Trevellick despatched a few bunches in his wife's hat-box, in due course receiving 7/6d. The next wholesaler he tried paid double, a tin trunk full sent to a third netted £3 – and this for a flower that most Scillonians regarded as a sweet-scented weed originally brought to the islands from the Mediterranean

William Trevellick (in the top hat), the pioneer of flower growing on the Isles of Scilly, at Rocky Hill, St Mary's, in about 1900.

The Woodcock family of Lower Rocky Hill, St Mary's, bunching narcissi in about 1880.

by returning sailors. Telling no-one, Trevellick went out by night with a trowel until he had gathered enough bulbs to begin growing them. Others copied him. The industry for which the Isles of Scilly are best known had been born.

Ironically, Augustus Smith died in 1872 in a Plymouth hotel bearing the name of his landlord, the Duke of Cornwall. As requested, he was buried at sunrise at St Buryan within sight of the islands he had devoted his life to. Once the news reached Scilly, a small flotilla of boats laden with sombre-suited tenants set off for the funeral. In death, he had found the respect that had eluded him when alive.

Augustus's will required the surrender of his lease on the payment of £20,000 by the Duchy and a further £3,000 a year until it expired. If the Duchy refused these terms, which it did, the islands were to pass to his nephew, Thomas Algernon Dorrien Smith, or Algy, then a young lieutenant in the Hussars. Initially, Algy feared that Scilly was beyond his means. His mother's family offered the capital he needed, and in 1874 he resigned his commission and moved into the Abbey. A year later he married Edith Tower, the daughter of Augustus's closest

friend, Lady Sophia Tower, who bore him seven children before dying in an influenza epidemic that swept the islands.

Algy's greatest gift to Scilly was the encouragement of the flower industry. He travelled Europe to study it for himself, returning to Tresco with new varieties and the knowledge that Scilly's climate gave its growers a month's start on their rivals. It was Algy who introduced the high protective hedges that still chequer the islands. By the turn of the century the growers were exporting 650 tons of cut flowers a year, and every scrap of available land had been planted with the Scilly Whites and Soleil d'Or narcissi *Punch* called Scilly's 'precocious gold'. 'It is flowers, nothing but flowers', observed one spectator to the scene on the pier when the Penzance steamer was being loaded, '. . . and by the time the hatches are battened down, and the deck cargo sorted up, the little steamer looks more like a Canton sampan than a sea-going craft.'

Algy died in 1918, to be succeeded by his eldest son, Major Arthur Dorrien Smith. By then four years of war had replaced the steamers with armed trawlers. St Mary's became a naval base, Tresco home to seaplanes flying anti-submarine patrols over passing convoys. The war led to the collapse of the flower trade, impoverishing the islands and leaving many houses in need of repair. In 1920, bowing to economic realities, Scilly's new landlord surrendered his lease and two years later agreed a replacement that left him with only Tresco. For the first time in nearly six centuries the Duchy had assumed responsibility for the day-to-day administration of St Mary's and the other off-islands.

Ten years later the Prince of Wales (later Edward VIII) arrived at St Mary's by flying-boat. By then the Duchy had installed its first Land Steward, built workshops, and pulled down and rebuilt much of the more dilapidated housing in Hugh Town. A Home Farm was started on St Mary's and the old lifeboat station converted into a bulb treatment centre for eel-worm, still a major pest. Not all these changes were popular. Scillonians had grown used to the Dorrien Smiths. The 'Major' was a bluff kind-hearted man who was universally liked. The arrival of the Duchy meant every lease being renegotiated. Some farmers found the new conditions so unacceptable they surrendered their holdings and crossed to the mainland.

The Quay at Hugh Town, St Mary's.

The man responsible for steering the Duchy of Cornwall through such potentially hazardous waters is its St Mary's-based Land Steward, Jeremy Pontin. He took up the post in 1993, building on the foundations laid down by his predecessor, Lieutenant Colonel Ian Robertson, who had done much to help bridge the transition from benign neglect to a more involved and active role by the Duchy. Jeremy Pontin arrived on Scilly from Hampshire, exchanging his duties as its County Estates Officer for a world ruled by the sea, and where the only methods are getting about are an old Landrover or the Duchy launch, the *Blue Dolphin*. The windows of his Hugh House office look down over two cannons facing out over the Garrison walls, across Hugh Town's rooftops, pinched on both sides by the sea, and away to the rising ground of the rest of the island. One wall is dominated by an immense multi-coloured map of the islands in his charge, showing each of the 350 farms, cottages, workshops, shops, offices and assorted other buildings owned by the Duchy. Much of

By 1949 relations between the Duchy and the Council of the Isles of Scilly had grown strained. Post-war Britain had no time for privilege. The Council urgently required land for council-housing, but was thwarted by the Duchy's exemption from the Acts of Parliament governing compulsory purchase. To appease its critics, and rid itself of a problem certain to grow more embarrassing, the Duchy announced the sale of Hugh Town. These were memorable days in St Mary's history. Over the next few years the Duchy parted with the freehold of 170 houses, 18 shops, 3 hotels, 20 boathouses and stores, as well as the cinema, steamship company offices, Roman Catholic church and power station. The results have not always been as pleasing as Scillonians might have hoped. Some houses were sold for a profit to 'outsiders', sowing the seed for their conversion to guest houses and the birth of the tourist industry. More democratic winds may have blown through the islands, but when the dust finally settled the Duchy and Council were left to co-exist in a complex two-tier relationship in which all but a fraction of the land still belonged to the Duchy, and Scilly's administration was placed in the hands of the Council.

Bill Burrow, the Assistant Harbour Master, raising the Duchy flag outside Hugh House, with Hugh Town's rooftops beyond the Garrison walls.

the balance, including the uncultivated land on the larger islands and all the uninhabited off-islands, is olive green. Since 1986 this has been in the care of the Isles of Scilly Environmental Trust, whose annual rent is a single daffodil.

One island, Tresco, remains blank. Following the death of the 'Major' in 1955, the island passed to his son, Tom, a Naval commander who immediately began modernizing its cottages and farming operations in an effort to make Tresco self-support-ing. Today, the island is leased to his son, Robert, who together with his wife and family continues to live in the Abbey – where the Prince of Wales is an occasional guest. Although the Duchy own the island, they have only a modest say in how Robert Dorrien Smith chooses to administer it. When he took over Tresco following his father's death in 1972 the family's trustees quickly made it clear that if the Dorrien Smiths were to remain on the island then ways had to be found to make it pay. The Abbey Gardens remain its greatest attraction, but in recent years a number of cottages and other buildings have been converted into timeshare accomodation. If an island's health can be gauged from the numbers attending its school, then Tresco's future is assured. At lunchtime, a flurry of children burst through its door, careering off on bicycles down traffic-free lanes: unlike the other islands, Tresco is still without cars.

Even without Tresco, Jeremy Pontin has ample on his plate. The flower farms remain the backbone of the Duchy's holdings, and his first and not always welcome task was to embark on a rent review of all fifty of them. Part of the problem lay in the Duchy's own *laissez-faire* attitude, which during the 1950s and 60s allowed island rents to lag behind those on the mainland. Another more serious concern is the fickleness of the trade in cut flowers, which is increasingly threatened by international com-petition, especially from the Dutch. Two-thirds of the flowers grown on the islands are today distributed by Mainland Market-ing, a co-operative set up in 1989 by two farmers, Andrew May and Keith Hale, with the help of a £50,000 loan from the Duchy. From October onwards, when the first flowers are harvested, right through to Easter, the company's purpose-built warehouse is fragrant with the Soleil d'Or, Paper White and Avalanche nar-cissi on which the Scillonian flower industry still depends. The

heart of the warehouse is its cooling room, where forced air draws the heat from the flowers to delay blooming. During the winter, supported by aircraft and helicopters, the refrigerated shipping service is tailored to the industry's needs, often setting sail from St Mary's early in the morning to meet road connec-tions a few hours later. Within a day of being picked, Scilly-grown flowers bring the promise of spring to florists and super-market shelves all over the British Isles. By the time the last of the annual 36,000 boxes packed by Mainland Marketing has been sold over the telephone to its network of wholesalers on the mainland, a total of twenty-two million flowers will have passed through its doors.

One of the farmers to supply Mainland Marketing is Jonathan May, Andrew's brother, whose 60 acre farm at Penninis is one of the largest on Scilly. In recent years, the higher levels of capital required have led to some smaller farms amalgamating, increas-ing the average size of those on St Mary's to 25 acres. In driving

ABOVE *Penninis Head at its most benign, with foxgloves in flower and Church Point in the background.*

OPPOSITE PAGE *A corner of the world-famous Abbey Gardens, Tresco.*

121

Picking Soleil d'Or on the slopes above Hugh Town, St Mary's.

rain and a south-westerly gale, white-capped rollers buffet Penninis Head. The oilskin-clad pickers stoop low over the rows, placing the still unopened flowers in baskets. From the fields they are taken by tractor and trailer to a packing shed, where a line of women deftly bunch and tie the flowers into tens, packing them into boxes. The bulk of the Soleil d'Or are harvested by the end of February, to be followed by the first of the daffodils. By Easter the harvest is over, and helped by machines the once backbreaking task of lifting the bulbs can begin. Part of Jonathan May's crop is exported to Holland. Some are discarded, some potted, the best used to improve the breeding stock

and fine tune the prospects for future seasons. The rest are sterilized against eel-worm, preheated in temperature-controlled stores and replanted during the summer. The bulbs are lifted in rotation over a three or four year period. Those not lifted are scorched in the fields with gas burners, thus triggering the start of the growing cycle.

Jonathan May is also Chairman of the Trenoweth Research and Development Station, once the site of the Duchy Home Farm. The Duchy charges the Station a peppercorn rent, for the Field Officer and researcher it employs provide a vital back-up to growers. Existing stock is improved to increase yields and lengthen the flowering period, research done into ways of reducing the use of chemicals. Over the years, the Station has also encouraged research into other flowers suitable for growing on Scilly, of which the most successful have been pinks, carnations, irises and gladioli.

A few yards from the timber-clad Research Station, in one of the handful of cottages that form the tiny hamlet of Trenoweth, lives the pioneer of pink growing on Scilly, Bert Whittaker. Bert and his wife Ruth settled at Trenoweth in 1980, successfully competing against 120 other applicants when the farm became vacant and the Duchy put it out to tender. Although recently retired, they still have a smallholding. The decision to add pinks to the potatoes, narcissi and daffodils traditionally grown at Trenoweth was an attempt to solve the single most vexing problem on Scilly: how best to stretch the flower harvest so that a farm's income is spread more evenly through the year. Unlike garden pinks, commercial varieties are recurrent. Even in mid-winter the shed in which the picked flowers are stored remains awash with colour.

Like many islanders, Scillonians are cautious of change. The willingness to take risks and try new ideas is more typical of those who have moved to the islands from elsewhere. The new tenants of Trenoweth are Francis and Christine Hosken, a young and enthusiastic couple from Cornwall who hope to add Kaffir Lilies to the other flowers grown on the farm. But the boldest attempt at diversifying in the recent past has not taken place on St Mary's at all, but on the remote off-island of St Martin's, where in a huddle of sheds close to the church five computer stations process the orders for 'Scent from the Islands', a mail-order business sending flowers by post.

Ten years ago, Andrew Julian hung up his Metropolitan Police Inspector's uniform and together with his wife, Hilary, walked the winding lane that leads from the quay to the island's largest settlement, Higher Town. Though both knew nothing of farming, and were uncertain of ever being granted a tenancy by the Duchy, they knew that the tenant of Churchtown Farm was due to retire. They offered to work for him for a year without pay, gaining sufficient experience to persuade the Duchy that they were worth the risk. The farm was windswept. Out of 26 acres,

Bert Whittaker watching pinks being picked at Trenoweth Farm.

Andrew and Hilary Julian in the flower-packing room, Churchtown Farm, St Martin's.

ABOVE *The Prince of Wales talking to Keith Low on St Martin's, during a visit to the Isles of Scilly in June 1993.*

TOP RIGHT *The 'Golden Eagle' gig-racing off St Mary's. The gig in the background is the 'Nornour', built in 1971 for a St Mary's crew.*

RIGHT *Richard Pearce in the rebuilt 'Golden Eagle' gig shed on Bryher, now his studio.*

only five were sheltered enough to grow flowers. Even with the income from letting the cottages that came with the tenancy they were soon losing money. Transport and freight costs – the curse of all off-island growers – were far higher than anticipated. Following on Bert Whittaker's example, they began growing pinks, selling them to the boatloads of visitors who land on the island in summer, and offering when necessary to send them by post. Eventually they placed a small advertisement in *The Sunday Times*, winning enough orders to meet its cost. Since then, the business has grown beyond all recognition. In the weeks leading up to Christmas, a quarter of St Martin's population of ninety-eight were found jobs working alongside the Julians in the farm's packing room. Before Mother's Day, 2,500 boxes of scented narcissi, pinks and other seasonal flowers braved the launch crossing to St Mary's on a journey that would end with them winning mothers' hearts all over England.

Many of the flowers so carefully packed at Churchtown Farm are grown by other farmers. The Julians would welcome more land, yet many of the fields on St Martin's have fallen victim to neglect and the cedar chalets put up in the 1960s to provide a second income. Recently, growers on the island have set up a Farming Interest Group to try and encourage more profitable use of the land. This 'do-it-yourself' approach has won Duchy approval, and they in turn have invested capital in a new glasshouse and farm building, converting one barn into an artist's studio and another into a cottage.

Scillonian barns are a delight. Yet architectural pride-of-place belongs to the gig sheds – alas now all virtually derelict – originally built to house the fast eight-oared gigs that once plied between the islands, and whose Victorian heyday is now celebrated by a succession of annual races between their modern descendants. Some were used to put pilots aboard ships in need of guiding to a safe anchorage, rival crews racing to be first. The fastest was the *Golden Eagle*, which owed its name to the American gold dollars, stamped on one face with an eagle, given to the pilots of Bryher after saving the crew of the American ship *Award*, wrecked off the island in 1861.

When Richard and Caroline Pearce first saw the *Golden Eagle's* home it was a roofless ruin buried in the dunes. The gig had

Jeremy Pontin, the Duchy's Land Steward on Scilly, admiring Peter and Sheila Miller's skill at rigging a fishing net.

fared better. After being sold to a Cornish pharmacist for £35 and restored, it eventually returned to Scilly and is now one of a select handful of veterans still used for racing. Richard was born on St Mary's, but had settled on Bryher to farm, a career he finally swopped for another equally precarious, that of an artist. Thanks to the generosity of an unknown cargo ship that shed 600 tons of timber during an overnight gale in the Western Approaches, Richard has rebuilt the *Golden Eagle* gig shed and given it a new lease of life as his studio, using timber washed ashore after the storm. The Duchy is about to begin the restoration of a second gig shed on Bryher, that of the *Sussex*, turning it into a waiting room for passengers boarding launches at Anneka's Quay and an information centre for visitors.

In summer, the first sight to greet many of those visitors is likely to be Peter and Sheila Miller, rigging and repairing nets in the field adjoining the quay. Peter is of old Scillonian stock. One ancestor was bailiff on St Mary's, his mother a Jenkins – a name dating back to the seventeenth century on both Bryher and Tresco, 'paying attention to neither Godolphin or Leeds, . . . owning the earth, disregarding the law'. Until retiring from flower growing, the Millers tenanted Vine Farm, which when they moved in in 1953 was the first farm on the island to break with the traditional succession of father to son. After nearly thirty years, Peter and Sheila abandoned the flower fields for their green bungalow overlooking the channel between Bryher and Tresco. When a passing trawlerman asked if he could mend his nets on their land, Peter offered to help. The pleasures of a less arduous life were put to one side as other fishermen followed the first. Today, Peter and Sheila are known throughout Cornwall for their skill, and though both in their mid-sixties are rarely without a net needing repair or a new one waiting to be rigged with its weights and floats. Remarkably, their charges must be the only ones on Scilly immune to inflation: the £10 they charge for each net has remained unchanged for fifteen years. This rich seam of differing skills is one of Scilly's most engaging characteristics. Everyone has a tale to tell, usually with humour. If it is prudent to bear in mind the editorial in the first issue of *The Scillonian*, the islands' magazine, which in 1925 warned of 'our trivial gossip and absurdly incorrect scandal-mongering', it is nonetheless as easy to be as seduced by the people as the place.

Nowhere is the combination more beguiling than on St Agnes, which together with Gugh forms the smallest of the off-islands. Rocks carved by wind and weather into tall fantastical teeth along much of its coast contrast with tiny high-hedged flower fields. A track leads up from the quay past the Turk's Head inn and post office, dividing near the school and now redundant lighthouse before looping downhill to the church and a second quay. St Agnes is Scilly in miniature, with the same wild beauty and unhurried pace. Yet as with the other off-islands, the gradual shift to an economy based on tourism rather than farming and fishing is bringing changes that aren't always welcome. There is the same anxiety that the growth in second homes may one day deprive the islanders of a home of their own, the same hope that the Duchy will not allow the need to provide the Prince of Wales with an income to make it any less benevolent a landlord. The Duchy's position is almost impossible. Scilly requires the most delicate and sure-footed of touches to retain the balance between the wish of some islanders to be left alone, and that of others eager to share in the wealth created by tourism.

One native of St Agnes not to have abandoned his traditional way of life is Kit Legg, who with his wife Natalie and three children live in a small cottage. For centuries the Leggs have lived from the surrounding seas, from piloting and potting. One old Scillonian sea-dog is reputed to have claimed he could 'plough and sow, reap and mow, and sail a ship with any man'. Kit is cast in the same mould. In winter he works alongside his brother in the flower fields, or helps Natalie manage their smallholding. But from April to November, unless kept ashore by the weather, he and his father, Herbert, spend their days at sea in the *Pioneer*, Kit's twenty-six feet long open boat, pulling the 200 lobster pots that earn him a living. The pots are laid in strings of twelve, and pulled, emptied and baited every other day. Like John Pender on Bryher, most of Kit's catch ends up in Spain. Each season the pickings grow slimmer. Bigger foreign boats prowl the rim of the three-mile limit. The minimum size of keepable lobster is constantly being increased. Though crabs remain common, lobster and crawfish are now scarce, with double the number of pots catching a similar weight as when Kit first started. A good day will see him land with 20 lobsters.

Alongside Kit's forefathers in the walled churchyard at Lower Town lie generations of the most celebrated of all St Agnes families, the Hicks, once described as 'masculine, untidy, litigious, given to fun, strong liquor and scandal, wielding a hoe for potatoes with one hand and brandishing a blackthorn in the other'. Happily, no such weapons are carried by their modern descendants, who still dominate St Agnes – and in more ways than one. For Francis Hicks and his wife, Carol, live in what must surely be the most prominent house on Scilly, the old lighthouse. St Agnes light dates back to 1680, and was the first built in all Cornwall by Trinity House. Both Francis's great-grandmother and grandmother were its keepers, and his father was born in it on the November day in 1911 it was finally put out. Francis and Carol farm thirty acres, of which only half is

St Agnes from the air, with Gugh in the foreground. The Turk's Head inn is the white building to the left of the quay. The old Lighthouse is the home of Francis and Carol Hicks, whilst just visible in the far distance, beyond Annet and the Western Rocks, is the most western outpost in the British Isles, Bishop Rock Lighthouse.

The 'Scillonian III' off St Mary's, photographed from just above the Iron Age burial chamber on Halangy Down.

Wreck extends to dead whales. A few years ago one washed up on St Agnes was blown up by the Army with explosives, scattering fragments all over the island. The lesson learnt, the recent appearance of a second whale on St Agnes's foreshore was treated with more caution. Coal, timber, and the Duchy's three-man maintenance team were sent over to the island. The resulting cremation took three days, leaving the next high tide to scatter the ashes.

The cost of two tons of coal is minor when matched against the £1.5 million recently spent by the Duchy on repairing and extending St Mary's quay. The original New Quay was built by Augustus Smith, whose nephew lengthened it in 1889 to meet the needs of the flower trade. By 1993 it was showing its age, and the outer berth, used both by the passenger ferry from Penzance, the 1,200 ton *Scillonian III*, and its smaller cousin, the *Gry Maritha*, which brings in all the freight, was in danger of collapse. Throughout the winter the residents of Hugh Town woke to the incessant thump of pile drivers encasing the quay in a jacket of steel piles, which divers then anchored to the bedrock. Once in place, the piles were faced with concrete panels deliberately made to resemble granite blocks.

Capital projects such as these bring little direct benefit to the Duchy, indeed the accountants who watch over its finances must have long ago grown used to the Duchy's income from Scilly being matched by its costs. Supported by the Prince's Council, Jeremy Pontin has now stretched their patience still further by insisting that money be spent on the Duchy's role as Harbour Authority. A disused storage shed on the quay has been converted into a waiting room and Visitor Information Centre. Moorings for the 2,000 yachts that annually visit St Mary's have been laid in the outer harbour, whilst those used by the islanders' fishing boats and launches have been reorganized and relaid.

In winter, only the lifeboat and doctor's launch hint at the bustle of summer. The *Scillonian III* lands up to 600 passengers a day. Lorries move to and fro between the *Gry Maritha* and Hugh Town. Foreign yachts, some carrying crews with an uncertain grasp on English, bellow for instructions. Launches crowded with holidaymakers slap through each-other's wakes, spray spilling over their bows. All this is the responsibility of the

sheltered enough to grow flowers. Despite such difficulties, many regard Francis Hicks as the best grower on the off-islands, proof of an unwritten agreement between the Duchy and its tenants that if left to themselves Scillonians are more than capable of looking after the land they tenant.

But the Duchy's responsibilities extend to more than the farmland, and in the recent past much has been done to correct past neglect, giving many the feel that a new and fresher wind is blowing through the islands. On Bryher, a redundant barn has been converted into a house, whilst a survey combining plans and photographs has been completed of all 500 barns on the islands, enabling the Duchy to plan ahead for their future maintenance or possible conversion to other uses. Until recently, household rubbish on St Martin's had been dumped over the cliff at Wine Cove – some of which ended up on the beaches. Aided by grants, the Duchy funded the clearing of the 200 ton tip and its removal by barge to Penzance. Some unwanted objects are less easily disposed of. The Duchy's ownership of the Right of

Duchy Harbour Master, Jeff Penhaligon, an ex-Chief Petty Officer whose unhurried calm comes from a career spent beneath the sea as a Naval sub-mariner. His assistant is Bill Burrow, the Duchy Boatman, who until recently was both the lifeboat's engineer and St Mary's auctioneer.

Though the harbour is Scilly's hub, its day-to-day activities occupy little of Jeremy Pontin's time. The same is true of the Isles of Scilly Environmental Trust. The Trust's Patron is Prince Charles, and its first Chairman was Robert Dorrien Smith, who to help bolster the £50,000 given it by the Duchy windsurfed the 45 miles from Tresco to St Michael's Mount to raise money through sponsorship. Its present Chairman, Humphrey Wakefield, is more than happy to remain firmly ashore in his pottery below the Garrison, but insists that the 'sweet disorder' of the uninhabited islands is an essential part of Scilly's character, and the lure attracting many of its visitors. Thanks to the Duchy, attempts to build a holiday camp on Samson in the 1960s were successfully opposed. Landing is banned on some islands during the bird breeding season, whilst shrimping and prawning are confined to the summer.

By placing the guardianship of so much of Scilly in the hands of the Trust, there were those who thought the Duchy had begun a gradual withdrawal from the islands. Time has proved them wrong. To some extent, Prince Charles's affection for Scilly has strengthened the Duchy's commitment. The Duchy may not be the paternalistic landlord older tenants recall, but Jeremy Pontin is eager to plough back its revenues into conserving the land in his care. One success has been the replanting of the miles of evergreen pittosporum hedging destroyed by the heavy snows and frost of a January night in 1987. The islands timber is also vulnerable, for most was planted fifty years ago, and a programme of planting additional shelter belts is now under way. Remarkably, the one tree to have survived unscathed is the elm, which on Scilly still flourishes, apparently immune to the disease that has cut so tragic a swathe through those on the mainland.

By far the most significant of the papers piled on Jeremy Pontin's desk is a recently completed report assessing how best to safeguard Scilly's wildlife and history. The report is a blueprint, listing archaeological and historical sites, suggesting land that could be brought back into production, defining wildlife habitats that could be improved or extended. Farmers whose land is included within the report will be eligible for grants, payable for ten years, to farm their land in ways which reflect the special environment in which they work. This closer relationship between the Duchy and its tenants is obviously for the good. Scilly's beauty is incomparable, its character unique.

Occasionally through neglect, more often deliberately, the Duchy has proved itself the best buffer against exploitation and over-development. But life is not easy on islands where the only true master is the sea, and it will need a sure hand at the helm if a course is to be steered between balancing the books and preserving the character of the islands. Scilly's most celebrated resident, Harold Wilson, once described his adopted home as a community in constant change blessed with the ability to adapt. A more telling portrait of the differences between Scillonians and the rest of us is the oft-repeated headline in the local paper: 'Fog in Channel. Mainland cut off'.

Sunset over Tresco.

Dartmoor

Winter can come early to Dartmoor, and a bitter wind swept the smoke from a chimney. A heron waded from the brook in front of the farmhouse, flapping away awkwardly over the valley. Behind the splash of red of the postman's van in the farmyard the land sloped uphill through small walled fields and out onto the open moor. In the far distance, Bellever Tor rose above a stand of conifers and the ruins of the 'Snaily House', where in Victorian times two spinsters added to their diet by salting down black snails, a habit local gossip mistook for witchcraft – whereupon 'their secret being out, the women pined and died, and the dwelling fell to ruin.'

The postman drained his tea, fought off the affections of a pair of sheepdogs, and bounced his way back up the rough half-mile track leading from Riddon Farm to the nearest lane. Inside the parlour, Margaret Norrish topped-up the kettle and put it back on the stove. 'We were snowed in for six weeks in '47. But we managed. Times were happier then. Everyone helped one-another.'

Her younger sister, Sheila, dressed for milking in overalls and gumboots, nodded agreement as a tractor driven by their brother, Richard, turned noisily in the yard and headed off to where their herd of beef cattle was grazing the sparse autumn grass. In the silence that followed, there was only the ticking of the old-fashioned clock on the wall.

At seventy acres, Riddon Farm is almost the smallest of the Duchy of Cornwall's twenty-two farms on Dartmoor. When Prince Charles visited it he stayed longer than expected, playing havoc with the tightly controlled schedule that guides his tours of the Dartmoor estate. It is easy to understand why. In its sturdy self-sufficiency Riddon seems almost to define a world and way of life – that of the remote high moorland farmstead. The granite longhouse, built to house the livestock one end and their keepers the other, dates back to the fifteenth century. About a hundred years later a second building was tacked on to the first. For generations, Riddon's tenants would have regulated their year to a seasonal calendar that barely changed, driving their chestnut-coloured South Devon cattle and hardy Whitefaced sheep along the tracks up onto the Moor, enjoying common grazing rights, the right to cut turf and gather stones, to take from the Forest 'all that may do them good except green oak and venison'. With their rights went certain duties: attendance at the manor court at Lydford, taking their corn to be ground at the Duchy's mill at Babeny, helping in the annual 'drifts' when stray cattle were rounded up and driven into the pounds at Dunnabridge and Creaber.

As a way of life it bred an independence of spirit that still endures. Dartmoor is not for the faint-hearted. Like most of the hill farms on the Moor, Riddon stands at over a thousand feet. The first snow can flurry in October, winter not end until May. Rainfall averages eighty inches a year. Sudden mists roll in without warning. The soil is thin and stony. Until the introduction of the subsidies and grants that support the modern hill farmer, a poor lambing or a harsh winter ended any hope of profit. When Margaret Norrish was a young girl growing up at Riddon in the 1930s, her parents scalded cream and made butter, sat

ABOVE *The tenant of Huccaby Farm, Dartmoor, Michael Mudge, outside a barn recently repaired and re-roofed by the Duchy.*

LEFT *Early morning on the Black Brook River at Oakery, Dartmoor.*

down to their own pork and potatoes, hand-milked their dairy herd, grazed a few beef cattle and twenty sheep on the moor. At harvest, a patch of oats was cut by a horse-drawn binder and thrashed for winter feed.

That same sense of frugal good husbandry has been inherited by Margaret, Sheila and Richard Norrish. Over the years they have reclaimed some pasture from the surrounding gorse. In the lee of one wall is a line of carrots, a few cabbages grow out of the wind in the shelter of another. Both sisters are spinsters, and though Richard is married and lives nearby, each plays a part in running the farm. Richard does the heavy work and drives the tractor, Sheila milks their twenty-five dairy cows, whilst Margaret keeps house and looks after the paying visitors who stay on the farm. Their father died in 1947. Two years later the Duchy fitted a bath and hot water so that they could add to their income by taking in visitors. Such is their hospitality that this summer one family returned to Riddon for the forty-sixth year in succession. The Duchy also paid for the dairy, and since its installation in 1961 Sheila has not had a single day's holiday or ventured

more than a few miles from the farm. She has no regrets: 'What would I want with Torquay? It's all here, on the moor.'

Yet the virtues that make Riddon so appealing are no longer typical of the Duchy's holdings on Dartmoor. Farms like Riddon have become increasingly rare as small farms are amalgamated to make them more viable. The Duchy of Cornwall is Dartmoor's biggest landowner, owning 70,000 acres, of which 50,000 is common land and 20,000 either farms or settlements. As well as the farms there are over 170 houses, 7 pubs, a quarry, 25 miles of fishing, the prison, 14 workshops, a bank, and the ranges and military training area leased by the Ministry of Defence. There are disused tin mines, archaeological sites, a pottery, pipelines, phone boxes, even the ruins of a gunpowder works. The entire estate sits within the National Park, which in turn means more consultation, higher standards, the balancing of public access with private interests in an area that has ten million visitors a year. The Prince of Wales has written of Dartmoor's 'wild beauty and remote character'. It is the last great wilderness left in southern Britain, boasting a history and ecology uniquely its own. From a distance it seems uniformly bleak and desolate, with only its tor-topped heights breaking the monotony. Yet parts of the Moor are surprisingly intimate. Oak, ash and beech tumble to fast-flowing rivers and streams. Tiny hamlets huddle against the wind in the more sheltered coombes. Islands of wild flowers grace the bogs in high summer. Even the emptiest sweep of moor is punctuated by a scrubby tree, which has somehow rooted in the foot of a wall.

Dartmoor's dry-stone walls switchback across the moors for miles on end, taming and dividing it whilst simultaneously holding the key to its past. Man first colonized the Moor about 6,000 years ago, since when it has been his activities that have had the greatest impact on its character. When the first Neolithic settlers built shelters in the clearings much of Dartmoor was wooded. Early man left behind enigmatic lines of standing stones, his burial barrows, the circular remains of his huts. At Grimspound, on a bracken-clad slope overlooking Challacombe Down, Bronze Age villagers surrounded their huts with

The Bronze Age settlement of Grimspound, whose circular wall encloses the remains of twenty-four huts and some animal pens, with Hameldown Tor in the background.

The Hurston Stone Row, near Chagford. The double row comprises fifty matching pairs of stones, of which the largest, in the foreground, is over six feet high. The Duchy and National Park Authority work together to help preserve the moor's archaeological legacy.

LEFT *A small moorland bog at King's Oven.*

133

a massive stone wall as protection against wolves. The Bronze Age marks the first great flowering of a culture on Dartmoor. Over sixty stone rows and 2,500 hut circles have been identified, creating an archaeological heritage whose preservation becomes increasingly important as the numbers who visit them increase.

It seems probable that Dartmoor's climate gradually deteriorated from about 600 BC, leading to a reduction in population. An early Iron Age smelter's workshop has been excavated at Kes Tor, where arable fields, sunken drove roads and house sites were also found, but from about this period to the arrival of the Saxons in the seventh century the Moor was largely unoccupied.

To the Saxon kings Dartmoor was a hunting ground, to their subjects a potential living where a wattle and turf hut might be rebuilt in timber as a farmstead was slowly forged out of the fringe of the Forest. Higgledy-piggledy tracks randomly linked one with the next. Trees were felled, terraces formed by ploughing the slopes to create narrow strip fields. As the better land became occupied, new settlers were compelled to push further up onto the poorer soils. The heart of the Moor became a summer grazing ground ringed by a network of lanes leading up on to it from all over Devon.

By the date of the Norman conquest a handful of estates and a larger number of farmsteads were scattered round the rim of the Moor. The only town of any significance was Lydford, where King Alfred had built a fortified stronghold overlooking the steep gorge of the River Lyd. The new borough, with its market, fair and mint, became the administrative centre of Dartmoor, a role it was to retain long after its commercial importance had waned.

The arrival of the Normans transformed the whole of Devon into a royal forest for hunting, subject to Forest Law. Its rule was harsh and punishments savage. Its laws upheld both the primacy of the deer, hare, wolf and bear within the forest boundaries, and the habitat on which they depended: the 'vert' as well as the 'venison'. In 1204 Devonian pressure – and payment – compelled King John to disafforest the county. Both Dartmoor and Exmoor were excluded, and the Royal hunting monopoly remained in place on both moors. Thirty-five years later Henry III granted the Forest of Dartmoor and Manor of Lydford to Richard, Earl of Cornwall, a gift that eventually led to it becoming part of the Duchy of Cornwall.

The creation of the Duchy increasingly formalized the complex system of privileges and duties that governed medieval Dartmoor. Some farms in the parishes surrounding the Moor acquired rights on it called 'in venville', whereby a small fee bought grazing from sunrise to sunset. A second payment purchased permanent grazing, as long as the number of stock turned out did not exceed those the farm could support in winter.

At about this time the first of what are known as the thirty-five 'ancient tenements' began to be founded in the valleys of the East and West Dart rivers. Most owe their names to the surrounding landscape: in Riddon's case the red of the heather on the nearby down, Merripit to the 'miry pit', or bottom, in the valley where it was built. Men like Wills de Meripitt may have been humble shepherds and stockmen, but they were also the Moor's aristocracy, free to graze their livestock where they pleased. They could pass on their holdings to their sons, who in turn could then reclaim and enclose a further eight acres of moor, or newtake, for a small nominal rent. Once Dartmoor passed into the hands of the Black Prince in 1337, they also became the Duchy's first officials: its bailiffs, reeves, moormen and agisters. It was they

Pizwell Farm, near Postbridge, one of the original 'ancient tenements' and first mentioned in 1260.

'Dartmoor Drift', 1877, by Arthur James Stark, the only known nineteenth century painting of livestock being rounded-up on the Moor.

who in return for a daily halfpenny loaf had to help at the annual cattle and pony 'drifts', events once heralded by the sounding of a horn at daybreak, driving any stock not claimed by their owners to Lydford, where they were sold at auction and the money paid to the Duchy.

The two acre pound at Dunnabridge still stands, enclosed by rubble walls and complete with a stone-topped shelter for its keeper. It is first mentioned in 1342, when 3d was spent on a new lock for the gate, and William Dunnybrigge was tenant of the neighbouring farm. Today the tenants of what is arguably the most gloriously sited of all the Duchy's Dartmoor farms are Marion and Roger Winsor, who keep sheep and cattle on the 625 acres of Dunnabridge Farm. A track opposite the pound slopes down past a hay meadow, which as a Site of Special Scientific Interest can only be cut after July when the rare orchids that bloom in early summer having finished flowering. Beyond the farm and its buildings the land falls away to where the West Dart river makes a lazy half-moon bend.

Marion and Roger Winsor's mud-splashed Landrover in the yard, and the lines of boots by the door, betray a couple whose farming year effectively begins with tupping in November, when

ABOVE *The walled circular enclosure of Dunnabridge Pound. The farm on the edge of the Pound was the traditional home of the pound-keeper.*

BELOW *Marion Winsor and one of her Dartmoor fillies amid the wild flowers and grasses that flourish in the hay meadow at Dunnabridge Farm. The smaller photograph is of the meadow's rarest flower, the Frog Orchid.*

the rams are put to their flock of 900 Welsh Mountain breeding ewes. Like their beef herd, the sheep are hardy and able to withstand the harsh conditions of the Moor. During the winter both cattle and sheep graze the three newtakes that go with the farm, only being fed with hay and supplements when the weather is at its worst. To the layman, the modern newtakes are indistinguishable from the open moor, but in reality they are enclosed blocks of land that form part of a farmer's holding. In return for an annual payment, the Winsors have a management agreement with the National Park Authority over the 200 acres of Bellever Newtake. No fertilisers are allowed and stocking levels are limited, thus preserving the traditional grazings of gorse, heather and moorland grasses.

In March the cows start calving, to be followed a month or so later by the first of the ewes. The entire lambing of 900 sheep, which even in an average year will double the size of the flock, is managed by Roger, Marion and one helper. To make the work easier, the sheep are brought down from the Moor to the small walled fields round the farm, known on Dartmoor as 'inbyes', so that Roger can keep an eye on them and help any ewes in difficulty.

Like many Dartmoor farmers, the Winsors rent some pasture on the edge of the Moor, where the lambs thrive on the richer grass. Their Duchy land is also divided, and much of the summer is spent moving stock from one to the next in a Landrover and trailer. June means shearing, a seemingly endless task that Roger takes on single-handedly, managing up to a hundred sheep a day till the last of the clip is finally bagged. In July the Winsors begin haymaking, whilst August brings the first sale of the new season's lambs. By the end of September most will have been sold, allowing time to sort through the flock to decide which to retain as breeding stock. By then the sheep are back on the new-takes, where the poorer keep encourages them to dry off from giving milk. The calves are weaned in October, and though they will be kept in for the first winter the rest of the herd is turned out onto the Moor. The year ends with the sheep being penned in the yard, so that each can be vaccinated before joining the rams in the fields adjoining the farm.

The bare bones of their year give no hint of the work involved, or the uncertainty of the rewards. A previous tenant of Dunnabridge went bankrupt, the nearest farm to their own has

Roger Winsor moving sheep in the early morning mist at Dunnabridge Farm.

been converted into a house. Without subsidies, high moorland farms like Dunnabridge could not survive unless the Duchy of Cornwall lowered its rents. A significant rent reduction would in turn mean the Duchy being less willing to use ten per cent of its agricultural income from Dartmoor to fund conservation projects on the moor.

As the owner of six Dartmoor ponies, Marion Winsor is a prominent participant in one such project, the scheme to improve the quality of the Dartmoor pony herd. The true-bred Dartmoor pony is a triumph of natural selection and the survival of the fittest. Canny, tough, able to breed and fend for itself on even the most inhospitable parts of the moor, the Dartmoor pony has gradually evolved from its wild prehistoric ancestor into what many visitors to Dartmoor regard as its most famous resident. During the nineteenth century thousands were annually sold at Princetown Fair and sent underground as pit ponies. Others pulled traps or costers' carts: yet more endured generations of small children bouncing in saddles on their backs. Gradually the wild herd became dissipated by cross-breeding with less hardy non-indigenous stock, producing foals unable to withstand Dartmoor's climate. The trade in horse-meat increased as the number of ponies on the Moor fell, from 30,000 in the 1950s to about 3,000 by 1980.

Like a former Prince of Wales, later Edward VIII, who in 1916 built up a small herd of high quality fillies and colts at Princetown in an effort to improve the breed, the present Prince became interested in the Dartmoor's future, adding his voice to that of the breeders determined to stop the decline in quality. Much of the impetus came from the late John Coaker, of Sherberton Farm, and John Pugsley, an Exmoor farmer and member of the Prince's Council, who in 1987 persuaded the Duchy, the Dartmoor Pony Society, the National Park Authority and the Ministry of Agriculture Veterinary Service to jointly initiate the Dartmoor Pony Moorland Scheme.

A knowledgeable eye observing the ponies in the scheme being rounded-up in October would quickly gauge its success. Any owner of an approved Dartmoor mare can enter, and the forty-five selected mares are enclosed in a Duchy newtake with one of three pedigree stallions throughout the summer. The foals born

LEFT *Judging the quality of the ponies entered in the Dartmoor Pony Moorland Scheme after the annual round-up at Dunnabridge Pound.*

BELOW *Anton Coaker driving sheep alongside the River Swincombe below Sherberton Farm.*

BOTTOM *Diana Coaker and a group of pony-trekkers fording the River Swincombe.*

RIGHT *Looking north-west from Combestone Tor, with Sherberton in the distance.*

the following spring are the farmers', with the colts forming a gene pool of readily available pure-bred Dartmoor stallions that other owners can make use of to improve their herds. In 1993, the scheme won the Duchy of Cornwall the Edward Morshead Award from the National Park Authority for its contribution to conservation and the enjoyment of Dartmoor's landscape.

When the scheme first started in 1988, the mares involved ran with John and Diana Coaker's wonderfully-named 'Higher Tor El Cid'. The choice of stallion was surely apt, for the Coakers are one of the great tribal families on Dartmoor, and Diana Coaker is well-known as both a breeder of ponies and the pioneer of pony-trekking on the Moor. A slight jodphur-clad figure, and at first glance formidable, her lopsided grin and glorious ringing laugh belong to a woman who has lived on Dartmoor most of

her life and who even as a widow still does most of her farm-work on horseback.

Sherberton Farm sits on a slope overlooking the River Swin-combe near Hexworthy. Sherberton is one of the ancient tene-ments, dating back to the end of the thirteenth century, and the remains of the old longhouse now house stacks of windblown hardwood, which her son Anton planks, dries, and sells as a high quality timber to furniture and musical instrument makers. Anton is the sixth generation of Coaker to live at Sherberton, carrying on from his father in farming its 1,500 acres. Once again, the traditional Dartmoor mix of sheep and beef cattle move with the seasons between the open moor, the enclosed newtakes, and the 'inbye' land closer to the farm. Their 600 breeding ewes are North Country Cheviot and Scottish Blackface,

both breeds that fare well on rough grazing, whose lambs are sold locally to be fattened on better land nearer the coast.

In 1909 Prince George and Princess Mary (later George V and Queen Mary) attended the traditional tenant farmers race-meet-ing at Huccaby. An old photograph shows the Princess in an outsize hat sitting behind the cups it was her task to present. Whilst the tenants lunched on sides of beef and plum pudding, washed down with Champagne, beer and cider, those racing mounted their ponies and galloped off on a course that included circling Huccaby Tor. For the third year in succession, the King's Cup was won by a Coaker.

Diana Coaker smiles at the victory. 'Huccaby Races was a great gathering point for everyone on the moor. They died out before the War, but we still have the cup in the bank.'

Riding is in her blood, and today she has 25 horses and ponies which are used for giving short rides on the open moor. But back in the 1960s they numbered nearer a hundred, local farms helping house the constant flow of children who came to Sherberton for her week-long pony treks. She was the first person to run paid pony trekking on Dartmoor, a move she owes to the then Dartmoor Land Steward, Colonel Roberts, who on a visit told her and her husband that they needed a second income to make ends meet.

As one of the two largest farms owned by the Duchy on Dartmoor, Sherberton's size would astonish the builders of the original longhouse. The first medieval farmsteads were more properly hamlets, each supporting from three to five families. In addition to their common grazing rights on the open moor, the five tenants known to be at Dunnabridge in 1305 shared a hundred acres between them. Some they farmed communally. The rest was parcelled out into tiny often scattered holdings: a portion of meadow, a strip or two in the arable common field.

Partly hidden by a grove of pines in the lee of Challacombe Down lies the remains of one such medieval hamlet. What at first seems no more than a jigsaw of moss-covered lengths of wall are the ruins of eight quite separate buildings. One has cobbled floors, another the foundations for cowstalls, several have simple stone windows.

The medieval farmers who guided their ox-ploughs along the ridge and furrow fields on the down above the farm held their land as tenants of the Dukes of Cornwall. Challacombe Farm is still owned by the Duchy, and in 1991 they commissioned a survey of the farm as a way of deciding how best to combine its management with the preservation of its historic landscape. For Challacombe encompasses much more than ruins. Within its boundaries there are hut circles, part of Grimspound, and four spectacular burial mounds, one of which yielded a Bronze Age dagger whose amber pommel was inlaid with small gold pins, dating it to about 1500 BC. The old field systems, with their banks and terraces, are the best preserved of any on Dartmoor. Remains associated with four centuries of the tin industry also survive, including the spoil heaps left by the miners and the leats dug to channel water for washing ore and turning water-wheels.

Thin winter sunlight lights up Challacombe Cottages, with Challacombe Farm just visible amid the trees on the left.

The tenant of Challacombe's 800 acres is Jeanette-Marie Cullum, known universally as Minn. Her enthusiasm for the survey helped make the Duchy's task easier. Despite reservations about her capacity to be guardian of so remarkable a legacy, her wish to limit the numbers of livestock on the farm to 'as much as I can comfortably cope with' makes her the ideal tenant.

For what the survey revealed was not just the importance of Challacombe's past, but the richness of its present. Its streamside pasture, old hay meadows and great sweeps of rough grazing embrace a whole range of habitats. Marsh violets and sundew, which digest the insects trapped by their sticky spoon-shaped leaves, flourish in the wet valley bogs. Skipper and copper butterflies range the open moor. The valley also serves as a migration corridor for birds, whose seasonal movements contrast with a resident population on the surrounding moor that includes ravens and the rare red grouse.

In consultation with Minn Cullum, and with the support of the National Park Authority, the Duchy initiated a series of schemes

Heather in full flower on the slopes of Headland Warren, not far from Challacombe Farm.

Dry-stone walling snaking up Challacombe Down, with part of the medieval field system on the left and the overgrown remains of tin-streaming in the gully on the right.

to help preserve Challacombe's history, landscape and ecology without placing the long-term viability of the farm at risk. Shelter belts of broadleafed trees have been planted, the stream rim left wild to preserve its habitat for wildlife, field walls close to the farm rebuilt to stress the contrast between enclosed farmland and the more open moor. The heather surrounding Challacombe is one of its glories, and as heather is under threat, not just on Dartmoor but right across Europe, it was decided to employ Minn Cullum's sheep to help preserve a 140 acre block of heather at Challacombe. By allowing her flock only to graze it during summer, the heathers on the high down behind the farm are already showing signs of improving.

Dartmoor in winter. Looking north-east from Two Bridges along the West Dart River towards Prince Hall.

Old records show that in 1842 a tin miner built himself a house and began farming the land adjoining Challacombe, by which date at least part of the medieval village had been abandoned. That same year, as part of the reforms introduced by Prince Albert, the regulations governing the grazing of livestock on the open moor were altered. The traditional ways of holding land on Dartmoor were changing, as were Duchy attitudes to an estate in which for long periods it had largely lost interest. To the Black Prince and his heirs Dartmoor had meant both pleasure and profit – its value for hunting and as a source of revenue from tin. By the seventeenth century the number of red deer on the Moor had fallen to below a hundred and the boom years of tin mining were temporarily over. Free of royal interference, the system

of enclosing eight acres on inheritance was widely abused. The eight became twenty, even thirty, on the grounds that rocks and bogs were excluded. Rents and dues remained unpaid as inflation reduced their value and made them less worth collecting. In 1425, Henry VI earned £110 from Dartmoor. Two centuries later Charles I received just over £25. Proposals for ways in which the Duchy might increase its revenue were more likely to line the pockets of those who put them forward. The Dissolution of the Monasteries by Henry VIII spawned a new breed of land-hungry settlers who were unafraid of enclosing what they could, usually on the rim of the Moor. Dartmoor's size lessened the impact of this gradual nibbling away of the open moor, but as more roads were built and farming methods improved so large-scale exploitation grew inevitable.

The Duchy's own lack of interest in its Dartmoor estate was partly to blame. By the 1780s the absence of a steadying hand meant that both the 'ancient tenements' and large areas of common land were being granted out to a handful of gentry, accelerating enclosure and the creation of newtakes. Amongst them was Sir Francis Buller, a Devon-born judge, who acquired the medieval farmstead of Prince Hall and transformed it into an opulent Georgian mansion surrounded by 2,000 acres. In 1791 Buller proposed that the entire Forest be enclosed and parcelled out amongst the tenants and holders of newtakes. The Prince of Wales (later George IV) first approved the Bill, then changed his mind, as Richard Grey, Clerk of the Prince's Council and the Duchy's Deputy Surveyor, marshalled opposition to the Bill on the grounds that its supporters were only interested in wresting 'every part of the Forest worth taking from the Prince . . . to throw off the Duchy yoke.' The Bill lapsed, and the Duchy tried to reassert control over the moor by revoking the traditional right of the holders of the 'ancient tenements' to enclose land on inheritance.

Fortunately for the Duchy, the next attempt to tame Dartmoor was mounted by someone whose interests tallied with its own. The only known portrait of the young Thomas Tyrwhitt shows a boyish open face as yet unmarked by the struggles ahead. Tyrwhitt was born in Essex in 1762, and first met the Prince of Wales when still up at Oxford – an encounter that led to his becoming the Prince's secretary. A seat in parliament, a knighthood, appointments as auditor to the Duchy and Lord Warden of the Stannaries were all to follow, but there can be little doubt that the memorial Tyrwhitt most hoped for was ultimately to elude him – the transformation of Dartmoor into rich profitable farmland.

Tyrwhitt first arrived on Dartmoor in 1785. Optimism, energy, and single-mindedness of purpose were at first on his side. By the age of twenty-five he had built himself a house, named Tor Royal in honour of his patron, and formed a 2,300 acre estate not far from Two Bridges. He planted flax, corn and turnips, hoping that others would copy him and new communities evolve, bringing wealth to both the moor and his employer. It was a foolhardy venture, and doomed from the outset. Tor Royal stands at 1,300 feet on as exposed and windswept ridge as any on Dartmoor. But Tyrwhitt made light of the obstacles. Land was reclaimed and enclosed. He improved roads and made new ones. Near Tor Royal he built some cottages and an inn, again honouring his royal master by naming the inn The Plume of Feathers and the tiny settlement it served Prince's Town, or Princetown.

Three months before the Battle of Trafalgar in 1805, at the height of the Napoleonic Wars, his new township acquired a purpose. 'Mr Tyrwhitt', reported a local newspaper, 'has suggested to the Government the propriety of erecting a building near Prince Town for depositing such prisoners of war as can be brought into Plymouth, and who can without difficulty be conveyed up the River Tamar and landed a few miles from the spot.'

An idea Tyrwhitt had been hatching for some time had been made public, and in the following spring he laid the foundation stone for what is surely Dartmoor's most infamous building, the prison. The origins of the prison's construction lie partly in Tyrwhitt's realization that his dream of transforming Princetown into a bustling market-town was illusory, and partly in the government's concern at overcrowding on the prison hulks moored in the Hamoaze and Plymouth Sound. Dartmoor's closeness to Plymouth and its wild emptiness were the perfect remedy, and a ninety-nine year lease of 390 acres was drawn up between the authorities and the Duchy.

The original prison compound was circular. Two walls complete with platforms for the guards ringed five three-storey accommodation blocks, a bathing pond, sheds for airing the bedding, a hospital, and market square. It took three years to build out of surface moorstone and quarried granite, the long winters bankrupting more than one contractor in the process. In May 1809 its first 2,500 inmates marched north over the moor from Plymouth, entering their new home beneath a stone arch inscribed with a quotation from Virgil, 'Parcere Subjectis' (Spare the Vanquished).

In reality, the 9,000 French and American prisoners-of-war crammed in the prison within a few years of its opening were spared little. Epidemics of measles and smallpox compounded by cold and malnutrition left 1,200 dead, to be buried in shallow graves on the open moor. Those who risked escape were either shot, bayoneted or thrown in the 'Black Hole'. Despite the hardships, the French carved exquisite models of ships and buildings out of bone and wood, which they bartered in the daily market for food and tobacco, and which today are much prized by collectors. Together with the Americans, they also built Princetown church. Officers were allowed to live outside the prison on parole in return for giving their word not to escape. Some courted local girls and remained in Devon after the war.

Whilst England was at war Princetown boomed. New houses filled the gaps in the broad main street laid out by Thomas Tyrwhitt. A mill and brewery were built. Napoleon's defeat at Waterloo was followed by peace with America. There was a final reminder of the old regime in April 1815 when nine Americans awaiting repatriation were shot by the guards in what become known as the 'Princetown Massacre', then the prison was emptied and its gates left unlocked.

Within a year, Sir Thomas Tyrwhitt rode down the lane from Tor Royal into what was already a ghost town, with grass growing in the streets. The prison's closure meant its lease reverted to the Duchy. But what to do with a purpose-built prison was another matter. Happily, the suggestions that it become an orphanage, or filled with pauper children from London in need of being taught scripture and how to grow and dress flax, came to nothing. Tyrwhitt was undaunted. Convinced that

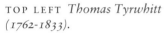

TOP LEFT *Thomas Tyrwhitt (1762-1833).*

LEFT *Tor Royal, the house built by Thomas Tyrwhitt.*

LOWER LEFT *Model of a French 'ship-of-the-line' carved in bone by a French prisoner-of-war at Dartmoor Prison.*

RIGHT *The church of St Michael and All Angels, Princetown. The church was built and decorated by the French and American prisoners-of-war held in Dartmoor Prison after it opened in 1809. The graves in the foreground are of French prisoners.*

ABOVE *Dartmoor Prison, with the television mast on North Hessary Tor in the background. In the foreground is a section of Devonport Leat, an artificial watercourse originally started in 1793 to supply water to Devonport docks.*

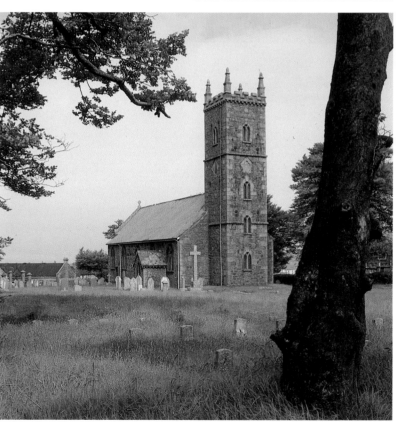

the town's future lay in improving its links with the outside world, he put forward a scheme for constructing a horse-drawn railway the twelve miles to Plymouth. Local granite, peat and flax would fill the wagons on the journey south, returning with fertiliser, timber and coal. It was a bold even speculative venture. The financial risks were considerable, the rewards uncertain. Tyrwhitt was undoubtedly eager to protect his own interests, but he was also an idealist whose vision of what Dartmoor might become burned as bright as when he had first arrived on it, some thirty years earlier. In a pamphlet arguing the railway's advantages, he wrote of his hopes: 'To reclaim and clothe with grain and grasses a spacious tract of land, now lying barren . . . to fill this unoccupied region with an industrious and hardy population . . . to provide employment and subsistence for the poor . . .'

The story of the 25-mile long single-track Plymouth & Dartmoor Railway is not a happy one. Shareholders defaulted on promised payments, costs spiralled, sections of the route proved so steep they had to be abandoned. Even after the line opened in 1827 it was beset by debts and the failure to attract traffic. Part of the track was eventually incorporated into the narrow gauge Princetown Railway, forming in its old age the route of one of the most breathtakingly beautiful of all railway journeys in England. But the line never showed a profit, and finally closed in 1956.

For Tyrwhitt, the original railway's failure marked the end of a dream. Tor Royal alone had cost him £47,000. By enclosing common land without compensation he had added to the hardships of Dartmoor's farmers, any one of whom would willingly have taught him the moor's most basic lesson: the need to work with not against it. Instead of 'clothing' Dartmoor with 'grain and grasses' he had built a prison and a drab incomplete town. To reduce his expenses the man George IV fondly described as 'my old friend Tom Tyrwhitt' moved to France, dying there aged seventy in 1833. There is a memorial to him in Princetown church, but today the church is empty and in need of repair and a more fitting epitaph is to be found in his obituary: 'and Dartmoor rewarded him as it has numberless others, who have toiled for nothing and left fortunes in its bosom.'

Tor Royal is still owned by the Duchy, and its 1740 acres are

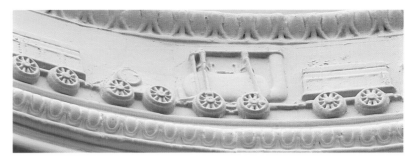

A detail from the plasterwork frieze commissioned by Thomas Tyrwhitt in the hall at Tor Royal to celebrate the coming of the railway to Dartmoor.

now farmed by Peter Crozier and his wife Anne. But Tyrwhitt's ghost continues to haunt it. Doors he brought from Carlton House open into panelled rooms. Beneath the glass-domed cupola in the hall a plasterwork frieze recreates the railway on which he pinned so much hope, its endlessly circling open trucks piled high with sacks and sheaves of corn. The two acres of Flax Field, now permanent pasture, recall yet another of his dreams. Another more costly legacy is the range of stone farm-buildings he built near the house, and which today require almost constant maintenance to be kept weatherproof.

Like Tyrwhitt, the Croziers are not Devonians. They came to Tor Royal in 1980 from a 100 acre Kent County Council smallholding. Peter Crozier is bluff and plain-spoken, and unafraid of taking the Duchy to task for what he perceives, rightly or wrongly, as its failure to support him when he first took up his tenancy. For the early years were hard. They had no experience of high moorland farming, or the sense of isolation many first feel after settling on Dartmoor. Tor Royal is the largest of the Duchy's farms on the moor, but size means little when farming at 1,500 feet, and Peter Crozier mentally quarters its acreage when assessing the quality. A framed photograph taken by one of his children during their first winter shows an Alpine landscape and sheep shoulder-deep in snow. Today, as well as their flock of 700 Scottish Blackface and Cheviot ewes, they also run 200 beef suckler cows. The better fields are all small, and unlike some Dartmoor farmers, who are virtually self-sufficient, the Croziers have to buy-in nearly three-quarters of their fodder and hay. The Crozier's holding at Tor Royal

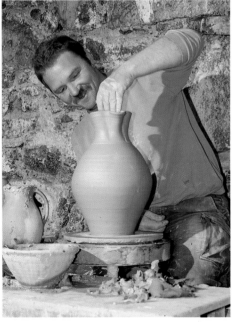

ABOVE *Children on an activity holiday with Spirit of Adventure, who are based at the Duchy workshops at Powder Mills, abseiling on Little Miss Tor.*

LEFT *Nick Collins on the wheel at Powder Mills Pottery in another of the workshops created out of the old gunpowder works.*

OPPOSITE PAGE *Powder Mills, looking west along the Cherry Brook. One of the two surviving chimneys from the gunpowder works can be seen on the right, whilst the buildings are now workshops.*

emphasizes the importance of livestock to successful farming on the Moor, a lesson men like Tyrwhitt and the other eighteenth and nineteenth century 'improvers' seemed unable to learn. For although enclosure continued and new farms were built, few remained profitable. A traveller crossing the Moor in the 1820s noted that 'the houses were shut up and falling to decay, the fences were torn down and Dartmoor was fast returning to its original uncultivated state.'

The whole problem of enclosure of common land was one that troubled the Duchy for much of the nineteenth century. Great tracts of land had been granted to absentee tenants at rents as low as 6d an acre, who in turn rented portions out for all they could get – forcing the commoners to pay for what was theirs by right. As landlord, the Duchy was held responsible. In response, its long-suffering first Secretary, James Gardiner, did what he could to soothe local disquiet. But the more he delved, the greater the abuses he uncovered. Buller's executors had paid no rent on his newtakes near Prince Hall for forty years. One farm had been sold and resold without records being kept or rent being paid. Tin prospectors and squatters had begun putting up rough-and-ready dwellings in an attempt to wrest a living from the moor, endeavours that were of dubious legitimacy and usually short-lived.

The truth is that Prince Albert and the Prince's Council never really formulated a clear policy for dealing with Dartmoor. Still remote and forbidding, no longer a source of any significant revenue, it mixed ancient traditions and Victorian opportunism in ways that made it difficult to pigeon-hole or police.

Typical of the new breed of entrepreneur was a Plymouth businessman, George Frean, who in 1844 set up the Plymouth & Dartmoor Gunpowder Company on land leased from the Duchy midway between Postbridge and Two Bridges. The roofless remains of the Powder Mills still stand, their two tall chimneys rising from an overgrown system of leats and reservoirs on the banks of the Cherry Brook. Frean's intention was to supply gunpowder to mines and quarries in the area, grinding the saltpetre, charcoal and sulphur in mills powered by the brook. The most hazardous process was the mixing, after which the powder was tumbled in barrels to make the grains spherical and

closer-fitting, adding to its density and consistency. It was then packed in barrels made on the site or compressed into fused cartridges. Despite an explosion shortly after opening, the mill soon had a hundred men on the payroll, one of whom ate his lunch and dinner simultaneously in case he was blown-up later in the day. An application to open an inn was opposed on the grounds that it would lead to 'idling and drunkenness', but one of the cottages served as a school and chapel. It was just the sort of enterprise to appeal to Prince Albert, who saw such ventures as a means of providing employment on the Moor.

The company's success was short-lived. About thirty years after Alfred Nobel's invention of dynamite in 1867 the mill-wheels stopped turning. In the 1920s the then Secretary to the Duchy gently rebuffed a request from two priests looking for 'quiet, loneliness and comparitive simplicity' to purchase the derelict buildings. Prior to the Normandy landings in 1944 the site became a training camp for American GIs, some of whom died from exposure despite burning what timbers they could salvage. In recent years the Duchy has done much to help preserve the surviving buildings, spending £50,000 over a five year period on conservation. The mortar once used for testing powder has been placed near the entrance, and the old cooperage where the barrels were made has been converted into workshops housing a pottery, a company making ground stations for weather satellites, and another specialising in activity and adventure holidays.

Amongst the quarries supplied with gunpowder from Powder Mills was one at Merrivale, a few miles west of Princetown in a valley rich both in archaeological remains and disused tin workings. Merrivale Quarry was first opened in 1875 by William Duke, and today is the sole survivor of numerous small quarries opened on Duchy land on Dartmoor during the nineteenth century. Its heyday was the turn of the century. There were steam derricks, a steam crane, a row of quarrymen's cottages. Traction engines hauled granite-laden trailers down the long descent into Tavistock. The quarry employed 150 men, who one year blasted 1,600 tons of stone in a single operation, some of which was used in modernizing London Bridge. By coincidence, many years later, in 1968, all 130,000 tons of London Bridge was brought to Merrivale before being shipped to the United States and rebuilt over an artificial river in the Arizona desert. To save costs, stonemasons shaved a four inch layer of stone off each of the 1,000 blocks from which the original bridge had been built, later shipping them to Arizona to clad a concrete replica. Only 30,000 tons of authentic London Bridge crossed the Atlantic, the rest was stacked at Merrivale, where some still remains, hidden beneath gorse and undergrowth.

Merrivale today employs only twelve. A sheer 200 feet high granite cliff, once the quarry face, towers over old spoil heaps and piles of newly cut stone waiting to be dressed. Merrivale quarries about 600 tons of stone a year, working it free from the natural beds in which granite is laid down in blocks of up to 200 tons. Inside one shed, a three metre computer-controlled saw-blade cooled by water from the Victorian leat methodically cuts 15 ton blocks into slabs, which are then reduced still further when needed. Some are used for cladding, lintels and curb stones, whilst yet more are hand-polished for use in monumental masonry. Recent work at Merrivale has included the Falklands Memorial, the Royal Air Force Memorial on Plymouth Hoe, and a memorial shaped like a pontoon bridge for Shrewsbury Abbey in memory of Wilfred Owen, the greatest of the First World War poets, who was also a Royal Engineer.

Six years after the first gunpowder left Powder Mills a much longer-lasting development took place: the prison reopened. A failed attempt to extract naptha oil from peat in the vacant buildings had again left them empty. The colonies were refusing to accept convicts sentenced to transportation abroad. New prisons were needed. Dartmoor's country air was deemed the perfect remedy for convicts who were sick or disabled. Old lags with wooden legs were amongst the 200 prisoners locked in its corrugated-iron cells when the conversion of the old dormitories into cell blocks had been completed in the autumn of 1850. Seven years later the numbers had risen to nearly 1,200, and the prison's reputation was beginning to change from that of a sanatorium into a dumping ground for the nation's most hardened criminals.

The role of the prison in the 150 years since it reopened is only relevant to the Duchy in that it provides it with an income and has brought a measure of prosperity to Princetown. In his 1992 Report into Dartmoor Prison's future, the then Chief Inspector of Prisons, Judge Stephen Tumim, began by saying that 'no prison has had a more melancholy or chequered history.' Although the image it conjures of working parties of pick-carrying convicts wearing fatigues stamped with arrows lives on only in the popular imagination, such is the prison's notoriety that the layby offering the best view of its buildings is rarely empty.

Since the 1970s the Home Office has allowed prison officers to live away from the prison, reducing the number of Duchy houses in Princetown occupied by prison staff. Twenty years ago, Princetown had a utilitarian air. No houses were owner occupied, and the entire village was either Duchy, Home Office or local council housing. All this has changed. The Duchy of Cornwall's aim to 'create a well-balanced and visually attractive village' may ignore the prison, whose presence dominates the village, and Princetown's climate, which averages 85 inches of rain a year, but much has been done to make it more welcoming. The Duchy has sold over 100 freeholds, investing £500,000 in improving roads and local services. Trees have been planted,

Princetown from the air, with Dartmoor Prison to the right. In recent years the Duchy has done much to make the town more attractive.

power cables moved underground, land provided for sheltered housing as a way of allowing the elderly to remain in the community. School numbers are rising, and, unusually for a village, it has a library and bank. In 1993 the Prince of Wales opened the High Moorland Visitor Centre in what had previously been the Duchy Hotel, and before that prison officers' quarters. The Duchy made the building available to the National Park Authority at a minimal cost, simultaneously contributing towards the cost of its conversion into what has already proved a highly successful Centre, attracting 150,000 visitors a year.

One of the clauses in the original 1850 lease granted by the Duchy to the prison required 25 acres of virgin moor to be reclaimed a year. By 1900 over 1,300 acres had been hand-dug by gangs of convicts working line abreast. Tree-planting was another task allotted the prisoners, adding to a gradual change in the landscape begun by Thomas Tyrwhitt, the first to realize that Dartmoor timber could both be grown as a crop and to provide shelter belts. One nineteenth-century Duchy bailiff planted 40,000 conifers and oaks, most of it felled during the First World War.

The shortage of timber during the War had an immediate impact on Dartmoor. The Prince of Wales (later Edward VIII), advised by the Forestry Commission, persuaded the Duchy to begin planting 5,000 acres of open moor as a way of creating employment and adding to the nation's timber reserves. The Prince's motives were faultless, the results less so. First Fernworthy, then Bellever, and finally Soussons Down, all of them rich in Bronze Age remains, and in Bellever's case the site of a medieval longhouse, disappeared beneath ill-suited stands of conifer – a process that accelerated once the Foresty Commission took over the management of all the Duchy's plantations and the outbreak of a second World War reinforced the need for home-grown timber. Like the Forestry Commission, in recent years the Duchy has grown increasingly sensitive when selecting sites for tree-planting. New plantations have been kept small, reducing their impact; large numbers of broadleaf trees planted to replace those lost in the severe storms of 1989/1990; and the high heart of the moor left open, emphasizing the sense of wildness so much a part of its character.

The arguments over afforestation underline the tightrope walked by the Duchy when balancing its management of the Dartmoor estate with public perceptions of what the Moor ought to look like. Nowhere are the arguments more conflicting or the lines drawn more sharply than over the continued use of 23,000 acres of Duchy land by the Ministry of Defence. The military use of Dartmoor dates back to a letter written in 1873 by Okehampton's town clerk to the War Office suggesting that the northern part of the moor might be suitable for artillery manoeuvres. Two years later the delighted tradesmen woke to the clatter of horse-drawn gun-carriages. For a month in August the boom of nine and eighteen-pounders echoed out over the hills to the south of the town. The Prince's Council in London shared Okehampton's delight. The boggy northern moor had defeated all attempts to reclaim and enclose it. Here at last was a purpose that would increase the Duchy's income, bring prosperity to the area, and serve the nation's best interests. The summer camps became permanent. On any day between May and September local peat-cutters might see a red flag flying from Yes Tor warning them of live firing. Infantry battalions joined the artillery for exercises. The area under War Office control slowly grew.

The outbreak of war in 1939 turned much of Dartmoor into a military encampment, particularly in the months preceding D-Day. Victory led to the beginnings of a debate about the future military use of the Moor that has occasionally been tumultous, sometimes simmered, but never completely died down. Feelings ran highest in 1967, when readers of *The Times* awoke to a front page dominated by a picture of the Chairman of the Dartmoor Preservation Association and 'shield of the moor', the redoubtable Lady Sylvia Sayer, defiantly striding through a turmoil of marines jumping from helicopters to fight a mock battle, her admiral husband at her side. Three years later the then Prime Minister, Edward Heath, announced that Dartmoor's days as a military range would soon be over. But nothing came of it, and the protests continued, reaching their height whenever the seven year lease between the Duchy and Ministry of Defence came up for renewal. In 1991, perhaps to extend the period of calm, the Duchy granted the Ministry a twenty-one year lease, subject to certain conditions: a reduction in the range size and the number of days when firing is allowed, the appointment of a Deputy Bailiff to monitor all exercises, and – most significantly – the ending of the use of high explosives by 1998.

The Duchy of Cornwall is in an impossible position. Despite the Ministry's efforts to illustrate the benefits to wildlife from the limited public access to its ranges, few can seriously believe that shellfire and conservation are compatible. The Duchy has stated that it would be pleased 'if at any stage the military are able to withdraw'. Yet the Chairman of its Council, the Prince of Wales, is Colonel-in-Chief of at least some of the regiments who train on the Moor. The Duchy's dilemma is obvious. It may privately look forward to the red flags being lowered for the last time, but for as long as the government of the day requires Dartmoor for military training it can do little but publicly support it. When granting the 1991 lease, the then Secretary of the Duchy, David Landale admitted that, 'finding a balance between the legitimate needs of this country's armed forces to train their men and women and the understandable but often conflicting concerns of agriculture, conservation and public access has not been easy.' There are compensations. A proportion of the income from the licence is used to fund the Duchy's conservation programme on the Moor, particularly such things as wildlife surveys and repairs to stone walls and traditional farm buildings.

Even the Duchy's sternest critic, Lady Sayer, has grown more sympathetic: 'People do cherish the moor and its wildness much more now. It's in good hands. I don't feel the need to put the armour on now.'

Dartmoor's Deputy Land Steward smiled wryly when the subject of the ranges was raised. After twenty-five years in the job it is a topic Colin Sturmer has grown used to. A bearded soft-spoken figure, the vagaries of Dartmoor's climate seem to have lent him the weather-beaten look of someone happiest out on the moor he serves. As Reeve of Dartmoor, he is entitled to a horse and green velveteen suit. In a box in the Duchy of Cornwall's offices next door to the High Moorland Visitor Centre are a few of the clay churchwardens' pipes once supplied to tenants at the Michaelmas audit dinner, when after handing over a half year's rent the farmers were treated to a lunchtime banquet in the Two Bridges Hotel.

Such customs stress the traditions that link the Duchy to Dartmoor. Leather-bound volumes of letter books stretching back to the 1860s line one room of its offices in Princetown. Framed notices record licences to cut peat, orders to 'immediately and on sight hereof to warn and summon twenty men'

to take part in one of the great seasonal 'drifts' of the commoners' livestock.

Even today, part of Colin Sturmer's time is taken up with the rights of commoners to graze stock on Duchy land. The old system whereby the four 'quarters' of the Moor were leased out to agisters at a fixed rent, who in turn took in commoners' stock and pastured them for the summer in return for a fee, has now lapsed. Responsibility has passed to the Commoners Council, of which Anton Coaker and Roger Halliday, Duchy Land Steward of the Western District, are both members. The numbers of livestock involved are enormous. Each of the thousand or so commoners who continue to exercise their rights might have hundreds of animals registered. As subsidies have risen, so have stock levels, adding to the pressures on the Moor. Newer cattle breeds are less hardy and require supplementary feeding in winter, leading to a concentration of stock in areas with the best access and leaving the centre of the Moor under-grazed.

As Roger Halliday's deputy, and the man 'responsible for the day-to-day management of the Dartmoor estate, from a leaking tap upwards', Colin Sturmer's main task is satisfying a Prince of Wales who has 'the will and determination to see that the estate

Duchy tenants on Dartmoor enjoying their churchwardens' pipes at the audit dinner in 1934.

Colin Sturmer (on the right) checking and loading equipment with his fellow members of Dartmoor Rescue Group.

is run in a right and proper way.' Twice now a ten year policy document has been drawn up stating the Duchy's ambitions for the estate during the decade ahead. The 'damn good shake' given it in the 1970s, and the arrival of a Duke of Cornwall with a genuine commitment to conservation, have meant Colin Sturmer being in his post through a period of change. When he moved to Princetown from Buckingham Gate in 1970, it was an appointment many regarded as a form of exile: the Duchy equivalent of Siberia. If so, it has been an exile rich in pleasures. He no longer lives in Princetown, but remains actively involved in community life on the Moor: as secretary to local associations, as Chairman of the School Governors, and as a member of the Dartmoor Rescue Group – the remarkable group of volunteers who turn out in all weathers to rescue the injured and lost.

The grant given by the Duchy to the Rescue Group is typical of the initiatives in which it has helped play a part. Over the years, young people have been taught dry-stone walling, disused farm buildings converted into workshops, 4,000 tons of gravel provided for a twelve mile bridleway. The Duchy owns the fishing rights to the East and West Dart rivers. At the Prince's request, ticket prices have been kept low, making the opportunity to fish their waters for brown trout and the autumn run of sea trout available to all.

Once off the Moor, the Dart runs south to Totnes, where it turns tidal and broadens into a wooded creek-fringed valley, reaching the open sea beyond Dartmouth and Kingswear. Throughout the summer the lower Dart is crowded with sailing boats slipping their moorings and hoisting sail before heading downstream with the tide. These have always been Duchy waters. In medieval times the people of Dartmouth had to provide a boat and four oars whenever a Duke of Cornwall wished to cross the river. Every merchantman that docked in the town paid the Duchy a fee once its cargo had been unloaded.

TOP LEFT *Fishing for trout on the West Dart River.*

LEFT *The River Avon, Devon, from the heights above Bantham, showing the river-bed, or 'fundus', owned by the Duchy.*

OPPOSITE PAGE *The mouth of the River Dart, with Dartmouth and the Royal Naval College on the left.*

Roger Halliday (right), Duchy Land Steward for the Western District, with Lionel Stribley, Chairman of the Cattedown Harbour Commissioners.

Today the Dart is one of four rivers collectively known as the Devon Waters whose foreshore and river-bed rights still belong to the Duchy; the others are Salcombe and Kingsbridge estuaries, the River Avon, and the River Tamar. In combination, the Devon Waters produce a sizeable income, which in the main comes from about 5,000 moorings, marinas, sailing clubs – as well as a number of smaller licenses. Day to day administration of each of these Waters is leased out, either to the local council, or in the case of the Dart to the Dart Harbour and Navigation Authority, who pass on ten per cent of their income to the Duchy.

Amongst the boats on Duchy moorings leased to the Cattewater Harbour Commissioners at Plymouth is Colin Sturmer's own twenty-nine-feet sloop, *Ginger Kake*, in which he and his partner circled Great Britain in 1992, completing the 1700 mile voyage in under a month. Once round Penlee Point, with the Breakwater and Drake's Island ahead, the pleasures of a safe return must have been tempered by the realities of the work awaiting. For Devon's Waters are his responsibility, taking up a

third of his time, and nowhere are they more complex – or remunerative – than on the Tamar and in Plymouth Sound. At Cattedown Wharves, the Harbour Commissioners administer the harbour dues, pilotage and mooring fees, again passing on a percentage to the Duchy. But the docks are expanding, requiring a further lease for any future infilling on foreshore owned by the Duchy. A second agreement is with the Ministry of Defence. Every Devonport-based destroyer dropping anchor in the Hamoaze does so on Duchy sea-bed. Its rights extend to the foot of the dockyard wall, making it easier to grant the Navy an open license to lay what moorings and beacons it needs.

The terms of such leases reflect the increasingly businesslike approach of the modern Duchy. It once owned Sutton Pool, Plymouth's medieval harbour, from where Dartmoor tin was shipped and the *Mayflower* sailed. Attempts to extract rent from wharves and slipways built on the harbour bed were constantly thwarted. The quay was lined with warehouses and inns, in one of which, the now demolished 'Three Towns', William IV, when still Duke of Clarence and serving in the Navy, spent much of his shore leave. In 1876 the Duchy admitted defeat, selling the 'water, soil and pool of Sutton' to the city for £38,000, a sum that took fifteen years to be paid.

There is no record of the Duke of Clarence ever venturing onto Dartmoor, despite its closeness, yet many of his brother officers have done so. A century ago, a trio of naval captains stayed in an inn owned by the Duchy, the Forest Inn, Hexworthy, describing it in the guest book as a 'very haven of refuge'. Today they would find it filled with walkers, bird-watchers, anglers, coach parties, families with children, couples out for a drive, foreign students hunched over maps. Unlike the three sailors, in need of hot toddys after a day spent 'wandering in such dirty weather as can only be found on Dartmoor', the vast majority of today's visitors remain within a hundred metres of their cars. Nowhere else is the Duchy so exposed to the public gaze, so mindful of the need to combine a working estate with public access.

A few miles from Hexworthy, at Postbridge, are the Merripits, survivors of a cluster of three farmsteads that date back to the Middle Ages. Higher Merripit is no longer farmed, nor does it still belong to the Duchy, but amongst its tenants was a predecessor of Colin Sturmer's as reeve, William White, seen bearded and booted and nervously fingering his bowler hat beside Princess Mary in the photograph taken at Huccaby Races in 1909. Not far away, and a stone's throw from the gloriously-named Muck's Hole Gate, is Middle Merripit Farm, where Kenny and Wendy Watson are now the tenants of its 800 acres.

Families like the Watsons, with small children, belong both to the Duchy's past on Dartmoor and to its future. Kenny's grandfather was a prison officer. He himself was born on the farm, recently taking over the tenancy from his father. Like most of his neighbours, he shares the conviction that Dartmoor's farmers are a race apart, that only they can make a living from the moor. This pride in being of Dartmoor stock, of farming the moor in the time-honoured way, is essential to the Duchy's

efforts to preserve its holdings. At Middle Merripit, footpaths have been moved to improve access onto the moor, new gates and stock-proof fencing put up, boundary walls repaired, stocking levels reduced to help maintain the fragile ecology of the heather uplands behind the farm. This is the Duchy working with its tenants in ways that at their best are truly a partnership.

Looking out over the Merripits towards Hartland Tor and the Bronze Age hut circles on Chittaford Down a sudden storm darkened the horizon. The sky blackened, rain beat down. It was nearly dusk. There were no cars, no people. Then a tractor pulled out from the yard at Middle Merripit Farm and headed off to where a group of sheep had taken refuge from the rain. Not just the Dartmoor estate, but the entire Duchy of Cornwall was in safe hands: Kenny Watson was getting on with his day.

Holidaymakers near Lower Cherry Brook Bridge enjoying Dartmoor in summer.

Acknowledgements

The possibility of attempting this portrait of the Duchy of Cornwall was first suggested in the spring of 1994. When I began the research, and Peyto Slatter embarked on taking the photographs that give this book its character, neither of us had any idea where our work might lead us, or how absorbing the journey would become.

The final book could never have been published without the support and encouragement of the staff of the Duchy of Cornwall, but I must make it clear that it is not intended as an 'official' history of the Duchy. Any errors are mine. The same is true of the opinions included in the book and the interpretation I have placed on the Duchy's history and the discussions that have helped shaped my thinking about its present. Nor is this book a definitive history of the Duchy, a task which though long overdue awaits a more scholarly pen than my own.

To list all those who have helped make this book possible is to defy a prudent limitation of ends to means. Our travels have taken us from Buckingham Gate to the Isles of Scilly, from Birmingham to Dartmoor. Wherever we have ventured and however improbable our requests we have met with nothing but courtesy. Our greatest debt is to Jimmy James, the Secretary and Keeper of the Records. No-one could have been more generous with his time, whilst his willingness to talk candidly about the aims and beliefs underpinning the activites of the Duchy showed a sense of trust we have both done our best to honour.

We are also grateful to Kevin Knott, Deputy Secretary, and to the Land Stewards in each of the districts, Roger Halliday, Tom McCaw and Jeremy Pontin. Like Jimmy James, all four have endured our questions with patience and forbearance. A special debt is owed to Kiloran McGrigor, the Duchy of Cornwall Press Officer. Her ability to meet our requests with humour and promptness has been one of the pleasures of working on this book. Other Duchy staff who have given freely of their time and detailed knowledge of its affairs have been David Curtis, Tim Gray, Christopher Gregory, Christopher Mathews, Nick Mould, Claudia Payne, Jackie Rogers, Colin Sturmer, Brian Wilson and David Wilson. We are also grateful to the Archivist, Elisabeth Stuart, for allowing access to the archives and illustrations in her care. A special thanks is due to the staff of the Duchy in each of its offices, all of whom have been as friendly as they have helpful.

Commander Richard Aylard kindly allowed me to quote the Prince of Wales's letter to his then Private Secretary concerning the Prince's wish to begin farming. Andrew Hamilton, the Poundbury Development Director, did much to explain the background to the Poundbury development. Henry Boyd-Carpenter's detailed knowledge of the Duchy's affairs over more than twenty years has been invaluable. Jo Draper read the first draft of the text, as always making many useful suggestions. Michael Havinden read the historical sections, again suggesting much that helped. The staff of the Cornish Local Studies Library, Redruth; the Local Studies Library, Plymouth; the Dorset Record Office, Dorchester; and the Minet Library, Lambeth, all generously provided guidance, suggesting avenues for research and further reading. Christopher Chaplin drew the location map of the Isles of Scilly.

Even a glance at this book will show that the Duchy's tenants stand full-square at its centre. Without their willingness to talk about their lives and work, and allow photographs to be taken, the book could not have been published. Many others have also helped with access, information, introductions, and the photography, and the list that follows calls the roll on innumerable small kindnesses, all of which have made working on the book a privilege as well as a pleasure, and to all of of whom we are indebted. If any names have inadvertently been omitted, the fault is ours, but our gratitude remains:

Andy and Jenny Atkinson, Nick Atkinson, Les and Dorothy Baker, Norman Baldock, Yvonne Bamber (The Prince's Youth Business Trust), Sarah Barnes, Keith Barrett, George Batten (English Heritage), Barry Bennett, John and Rosemary Berry, Roy Bishop, Mike Boulton (A&G Aviation, Bournemouth), Dave Brewer, L. J. Bullen, Bill Burrow, Andrew Carthew, Amanda Chalmers, Diana and Anton Coaker, Dick Cobb, Nick Collins, Andrew and Peter Cooke, Eric and Gladys Comley, Mike Cornish, Andrew Council, Colin and Myrene Coward, Augusta Creagh-

Osborne, Robert Crever, Charles Crichton, Peter and Anne Crozier, Minn Cullum, Dartmoor National Park Authority, Andrew Davis, Ben Deeble, John Diplock, Robert Dorrien Smith, John Down, Andy and Margaret Duncan, Brian Easterbrook, Martin Eddy, Trevor Edwards (Cornwall Wildlife Trust), Richard England, Roy Evans, Lisa Fagan (Surrey County Cricket Club), Nick and Victoria Finding, Paul and Peggy Foster, Eddie and Philip Fry, Hugh Gay, Frank Gibson, Judy Gordon-Jones, The Governor, H.M.Prison, Dartmoor, Roy and Joyce Graham, Tom Greeves, Marie Haddleton, Keith Hale, Leslie and Dorothy Hardwick, Ron and Valerie Hardwick, Colin and Marilyn Hawkins, Frank and Nan Heath, Walter Hibberd, Francis and Carol Hicks, Len Hodges, Laurence Holmes, Clive and Rex Hooper, Michael and Margaret Hooper, Jim Hopwood, Peter and Christine Hopwood, Michael Horrell, Francis and Christine Hosken, John and Hilary Hoskin, Gladys Hughes, Sheena Hughes, Moira Hulett, Alan Humphries, Dennis Hutchings, Peter Jeffery, Len Jenkins, Andrew Jones, Simone Jones, Andrew and Hilary Julian, Roger Keedle, Mary Kent, Keith Kellaway (Dorchester Town Football Club), Graham and Kate Kitto, Jack and Margaret Lake, Ian Lamb, Andrew Lawson, Katrina Legg, Kit and Natalie Legg, Lawrence and Brenda Light, Mervyn Lillicrap, John Lister, Guy Lock, Peter Lock, James Long, Terence de Lury, Geoffrey Maddever, Frank and Sue Martin, John, Margaret and Mark Menhinick, Andrew May, Jonathan May, Peter and Sheila Miller, Andrew Morton, Don Moxom, Ian Mugridge (Exeter Flying Club), Hamish Murray, Mike Nelhams, John Nicholls, Sheila, Margaret and Roger Norrish, Richard Olivier, Carol Omar, Rodney Osborne, Steve and Julia Ottery, Steve Parsons, Bob, Simon and Judith Peach, Richard and Caroline Pearce, John Pender, Malcolm and Eileen Persey, Ian Piper, Plymouth Sound Branch of the British Sub-Aqua Club, Powell and Jean Price, John Pugsley, Molly Rennie, Rob and Gill Reskelly, Peter Rose, Serena Rouse, Peggy Rowe (Radstock Museum), Steve Scoffin, Ruth Seber, Sandy Simpson, Jack Sims, Ian Skelton, Robin and Gillian Snelson, Jane Spiers, Lionel Stribley, Malcolm Thomas, John Tovey, Hilary Townsend, Graham and Sandra Vallis, Mike Vigar (The Isles of Scilly Skybus Ltd), Humphrey Wakefield, Steve Walker, Bert Watley, Kenny and Wendy Watson, John Weir, Bert and Ruth Whittaker, Brian Wilkinson, Roger and Marion Winsor, Richard Wood, Diana Wynne.

The Illustrations

Virtually all of the photographs were specially taken by Peyto Slatter over a two year period. We are, however, grateful to the following for allowing the reproduction of illustrations which are in their posession or for which they own the copyright: The Royal Collection, Her Majesty The Queen, page 31; The Duchy of Cornwall, 1, the map on page 11, 14, 25 top, 28, 29, 34, 41 right, 42, 44, 45, 46,57, 86, 91, 93, 97 top, 98, 99 left, 144 top left, 150 left; The Royal Albert Museum and Art Gallery, Exeter, 135; The British Library (Cotton Nero DV1 f.31), 17; The British Museum, 365 right; A.G.Carrick Ltd (Andrew Lawson) 64, 65 top, 66 bottom; The Dorset Natural History and Archaeological Society, Dorset County Museum, 107; J.W.Evans & Sons Ltd, 101; Frank Gibson, 116 left, 117, 118, 122; Harry Graham, 124 left; Mark Groves, 112; The Ironbridge Gorge Museum, 33; The Isles of Scilly Museum, 113 top; London Borough of Lambeth Archives Department 89, 92 right, 95 top & bottom, 96 right; Brian Moody (Duchy of Cornwall) 47; The National Portrait Gallery, 24; Radstock, Midsomer Norton & District Museum Society, 38; Walkers Shortbread Ltd, 56 left; Martin Warren, 88; Arthur Wills and Tony Bawden, 21; Woodmansterne, 22;

Select Bibliography

Allsop, Niall, *The Somersetshire Coal Canal Rediscovered*, 1988

Barber, Richard, *Edward, Prince of Wales and Aquitaine*

Brooking-Rowe, J., *Sir Thomas Tyrwhitt and Princetown*, 1905

Bush, Robin, *Somerset, The Complete Guide*, 1994

Coate, Mary, *The Duchy of Cornwall, Its History and Administration*, Transactions of the Royal Historical Society 1927

Coote, Stephen, *A Play of Passion, The Life of Sir Walter Raleigh*, 1993

Cornwall Archaeological Unit, *Former Industrial Sites in the Ownership of the Duchy of Cornwall*, 1989

Crossing, William, *Hundred Years on Dartmoor*, edited and with an introduction by Brian Le Messurier, 1967

Dawson, Graham. J., *The Black Prince's Palace at Kennington*, British Archaeological Reports 26, 1976

Devon & Cornwall Record Society, *Parliamentary Survey of the Duchy of Cornwall*, Parts I & II, edited by Norman J.G.Pounds, 1982/1984

Dimbleby, Jonathan, *The Prince of Wales, A Biography*, 1994

Down, C.J. & Warrington, A.J., *The History of the Somerset Coalfield*

Edelstein, T.J., *Vauxhall Gardens*, catalogue to Exhibition at Yale Centre for British Art, 1983

Emerson, Barbara, *The Black Prince*, 1976

Exeter Museums Archaeological Field Unit (A.R.Pye & R.Robinson), *An Archaeological Survey of the Gunpowder Factory at Powdermills Farm*, 1990

Garbett, Geoff & Skelton, Ian, *The Wreck of the Metta Catharina*, 1987

Gill, Crispin, *The Isles of Scilly*, 1975
   edited by, *Dartmoor, A New Study*, 1970
   edited by, *The Duchy of Cornwall*, 1987

Gray, Todd (and others), *Tudor and Stuart Devon*, 1994

Haddleton, Marie, *The Jewellery Quarter*, 1987

Haining, Peter, *Charlie Chaplin, A Centenary Celebration*, 1989

Hansford Worth, R., *Worth's Dartmoor*, 1967

Harris, Helen, *Industrial Archaeology of Dartmoor*, 1968, 1986

Haslam, Graham, *An Administrative Study of the Duchy of Cornwall 1500-1650*, 1980

Hatcher, J., *Rural Economy and Society in the Duchy of Cornwall 1300-1500*, 1970

Hemery, Eric, *High Dartmoor*, 1983

Henderson, Charles, *Essays in Cornish History*, 1935

H.R.H. The Prince of Wales, *A Vision of Britain*, 1989

H.R.H. The Prince of Wales & Clover, Charles, *Highgrove, Portrait of an Estate*, 1993

Hobhouse, Hermione, *Prince Albert, His Life and Work*, 1983

Hoskins, W.G., *Devon*, 1954, 1972

Howarth, Patrick, *George VI*, 1987

Inglis-Jones, Elisabeth, *Augustus Smith of Scilly*, 1969

James, Trevor, *A Glimpse of Dartmoor Prison*, 1995

Judd, Denis, *The Life and Times of George V*, 1973

Lady Margaret Hall Settlement, *Social Services in North Lambeth and Kennington*, 1939

Lemmon, David, *The History of Surrey County Cricket Club*, 1989

Montgomery, H.H., *History of Kennington*, 1889

Moule, Henry, *Eight Letters to Prince Albert*, 1855

Mumford, Clive, *Portrait of the Isles of Scilly*, 1967

Nicholson, Harold, *George V. His Life and Reign*, 1952

Pope-Hennessy, James, *Queen Mary*, 1959

Rhodes-James, Robert, *Prince Albert, Consort*, 1983

Rowe, John, *Cornwall in the Age of the Industrial Revolution*, 1953, 2nd ed 1993

Rowse, A.L., *Tudor Cornwall*, 1941
   'The Duchy of Cornwall', *West Country Stories*, 1945

Skinner, John, *Journal of a Somerset Rector 1803-1834*, 1930

Stanbrook, Elisabeth, *Dartmoor Forest Farms*, 1994

Survey of London, Part I, Vol XXIII, 1951
   Part II, Vol XXVI

Thomas, Charles, *Explorations of a Drowned Landscape*, 1985

Ziegler, Philip, *King Edward VIII*, 1990